The Uniforms of 1798–1803

Yeomanry Cavalry Officer

Armed Insurgent

The Uniforms of 1798–1803

F. GLENN THOMPSON

With a foreword by
Major General Patrick F. Nowlan

FOUR COURTS PRESS

This book was typeset
in 10.5 on 13.5 pt Ehrhardt for
FOUR COURTS PRESS
Fumbally Lane, Dublin 8, Ireland
e-mail: info@four-courts-press.ie
and in North America
FOUR COURTS PRESS
c/o ISBS 5804 N.E. Hassalo Street, Portland, OR 97213.

A catalogue record for this title
is available from the British Library.

ISBN   1–85182–393–x hbk
1–85182–396–4 pbk

Printed in Spain by Estudios Gráficos Zure, Bilbao

FOREWORD

For several years, many of my colleagues and I have been aware of the excellent illustrations of military uniforms and rank insignia, badges etc. that Glenn Thompson has produced for various publications including *An Cosantóir*, the Irish Defence Journal. The National Museum of Ireland, also, has availed itself of his skills and special knowledge of military dress and weaponry associated with the history of war in Ireland and Irishmen at war. His long service on the Council of the Military History Society of Ireland is indicative of his passionate interest in Ireland's military heritage. That interest, which extends beyond the island to wherever Irish soldiers marched, has brought him international recognition. I hope that, in the not too distant future, his expertise will be available to make a contribution to the presentation of Ireland's military heritage in an all-Ireland military museum in Dublin.

This is a unique publication in this bicentenary of the '98 rebellion. Here, for the first time, illustrations of the uniforms of rebels, yeomanry, militia, as well as pikes, muskets and artillery, are made available in a single volume. This work, combining the visual with descriptive narratives, provides for the general reader and specialist alike an essential compendium of the dress and main weaponry of the various combatants in 1798. The purpose of this volume is not to make judgments or observations on the events of that fateful year but simply to present pictorially the United Irishmen, the militia and the yeomanry, all of which were established in the 1790s.

Among the illustrations is an excellent example of a six-pounder gun. This was one of the most effective pieces of artillery in the 18th and 19th centuries. It was so much admired by the eminent soldier and gunner – Napoleon Bonaparte – that he copied it from the British and had it manufactured in France in 1803. During 1798 the rebels used it, and other guns that they had captured, whenever gunpowder was available. Former members of the militia, who had learned the gunner's trade with the Royal Irish Artillery Regiment at Chapelizod, Dublin, frequently provided the expertise in gunnery for the forces of the United Irishmen.

Glenn Thompson has family connections with Wexford town and a life-long interest in the history of the county. As a 'Yellabelly' with an interest in military history I was delighted when the plans for this publication were first proposed a few years ago. My enthusiasm for the project increased when I saw some of the early drawings. It is a great pleasure to see that the excellent results of the painstaking attention to detail, the toil and the dedication of Glenn Thompson have been recognised by the publishers and will be made available to the public. It is an essential reference book for libraries, museums and for anyone interested in local history.

Patrick F. Nowlan,
Major General

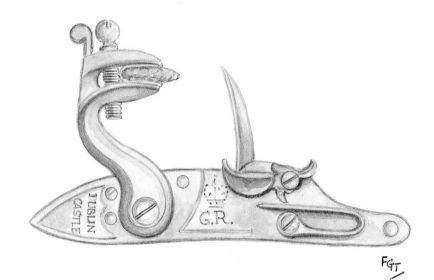

The flintlock mechanism of
the Brown Bess musket
(an example bearing the stamp of Dublin Castle)

PREFACE

About four years ago I began to realise that the bicentenary of the 1798 Insurrection was on the horizon. It occurred to me that many books commemorating this important event in Irish history had and would be published, but none had documented the uniforms worn by the various forces involved during that epic period.

On one of my numerous visits to the National Museum, I inspected a coat worn by an officer of the Antrim Militia. From this I made rough sketches; these in turn led to a proper colour plate and from that exercise the idea developed to record and illustrate what was worn and used during the years 1798 to 1803.

I am mindful of the advice I received over thirty-five years ago from the late William A. Thorburn, Keeper of the Scottish United Services Museum from 1955 to 1982, to whom I pay tribute; he told me that in the study of military uniforms, the most accurate source of information is the uniform itself. Fortunately some have survived the ravages of time and these are recorded in the following pages.

I should like to thank in the first place, my wife Iris, to which this book is dedicated, and without whose encouragement right from its inception it would not have seen the light of day. Words cannot express my gratitude.

A special word of thanks must go to Dr Con Costello, Tom McCaughren and Major General P.F. Nowlan for their personal interest and invaluable help.

I would also like to express my grateful thanks to the following who have so willingly helped me in many ways with this project: David Carberry, Wexford County Museum, Enniscorthy; Colleen Dube; Dr Kenneth P. Ferguson; Jim Hogan; the late Pat Johnston, Civic Museum, Dublin; Robert Jones; Jacques Lekeu; Patrick Long, Monaghan County Museum, Monaghan; Pat Murray; Niamh O'Sullivan, Kilmainham Jail Museum, Dublin; the Earl of Roden; the Rev. Jack Robinson; Padráig Ó Snodaigh; Jasper Tyrrell; Stephen Wood, Scottish United Services Museum, Edinburgh; Tom Wylie, Ulster Museum, Belfast; Ms Alex Ward, Grand Lodge of Freemasons of Ireland Museum, Dublin; Paul Doyle, Mairead Dunleavy, Lar Joye and Michael Kenny, all of the National Museum of Ireland, Collins Barracks, Dublin, who over the years have made available to me uniforms, headdress and associated items which have enabled me to have first-hand and accurate knowledge of the actual pieces; Inez Fletcher and Colette O'Daly of the National Library of Ireland, Dublin, for locating valuable sources of documentation; Séamus Corballis and Joe McDonnell for their knowledge in the study of military buttons; Brigadier General P.D. Hogan, President, Military History Society of Ireland and to the following members of the Council of the Society: Lieut. Colonel J.P. Coyle, Dr Sean Duffy, Comdt. Joe Gallagher, Capt. Padraic Keane, Comdt. Eamon Kiely, Comdt. Martin Lenihan, Comdt. Frank McGoldrick, Dr Pat McCarthy, Brigadier General Colm Mangan, Dr Sheila Mulloy, Dr Harman Murtagh, Comdt. Louis O'Brien, Colonel Donal O'Carroll, Brigadier General Patrick Purcell and Comdt. Peter Young, to whom I owe deep gratitude for their interest and support. And finally, but my no means least to my friend and good neighbour Dorothy Brown, who undertook so willingly and efficiently the preparation of the typescript, thus saving me many extra hours work.

F. Glenn Thompson

TO IRIS WITH LOVE

CONTENTS

The ill-fated expedition to Bantry Bay in December 1796 under the command of General Lazare Hoche included an Irish Legion or Légion Irlandaise, which he raised from remnants of the Irish Brigade of the *ancien régime* in 1790. Hoche's expedition was the first of several attempts to achieve Irish independence during this revolutionary period.

Red coats were a characteristic of foreign regiments in the service of the kings of France, whereas white was the standard colour for Infantry of the Line. The uniforms which survived the Revolution in France were utilised for service by the Republic. The Légion Irlandaise was clothed in red coats, most likely from what survived from the former Irish Brigade. Had Hoche's expedition proved a success, red coats would once again have faced red on the field of battle as they had at Fontenoy in 1745. This Irish Legion[1] was disbanded on 21 February 1799.

A **fusiler** in the French Army was a private soldier of the centre company, as distinct from elite soldiers of the grenadier and voltigeur companies. (The term *fusil* in French referred to a musket.) The fusilier wore a black felt tricorn hat, often worn according to individual taste, with a red carrot-shaped pompom. Below this device was a circular cockade, bearing the colours of the Republic, blue, white and red, held in place by a white loop and a small white metal button. The coat was red with a green stand collar, cuffs, lapels, turnbacks and piping on both cuffs and shoulder straps. There were variations to the style of collar during the early years of the Republic. All the buttons on the coat and waistcoat were white metal. Each lapel had a row of six large buttons at the edge with a single button at the top point. A further three buttons were placed on the right edge of the coat below the lapel. The small buttons on the red shoulder straps (shoulder straps were a plain type of epaulette without tufts or fringes) were placed at the shoulder end of the men's coats. Each cuff patch carried three small buttons. Breeches and waistcoat were white. Black leggings were worn above the knee; these had a row of small pewter buttons on each side. The shoes were of black leather. The single white shoulder belt usually had a black leather ammunition pouch attached at the rear and also carried the bayonet in its brown leather scabbard in a white frog on the right side. The white straps worn under the shoulder straps held a skin knapsack at the back.

The main armament was the **1777 model musket**, which had a somewhat more slender stock than its British counterpart; the barrel was reinforced with two metal rings. A white sling was normally carried. The steel bayonet had a cylindrical socket which was placed over the end of the musket barrel and secured with a locking ring.

The **officer** wore the same type of hat as the fusilier, but with a plume in the national colours; the cockade was held by a silver lace loop and a small silver button. The red coat was similar to that already described except that the cut-away stand collar exposed a black stock. Once again there were variations to collars and coats. Silver-lace epaulettes were worn on both shoulders, but junior officers wore fringed epaulettes on the left shoulder only; senior officers wore fringed epaulettes on both. All buttons on the coat and waistcoat were silver. Breeches and waistcoat were white. The black leather boots had tan top portions with small straps at each side. The sword was the type carried by officers of fusilier or centre companies; the blade was straight, and the hilt and guard were white metal with a silver-lace sword knot; the black scabbard had white metal mountings. A white leather frog, suspended from a belt worn under the waistcoat, held the scabbard in place.

---

1 Not to be mistaken for Napoleon's Irish Legion, formed in 1803.

PLATE 1
LÉGION IRLANDAISE, 1796

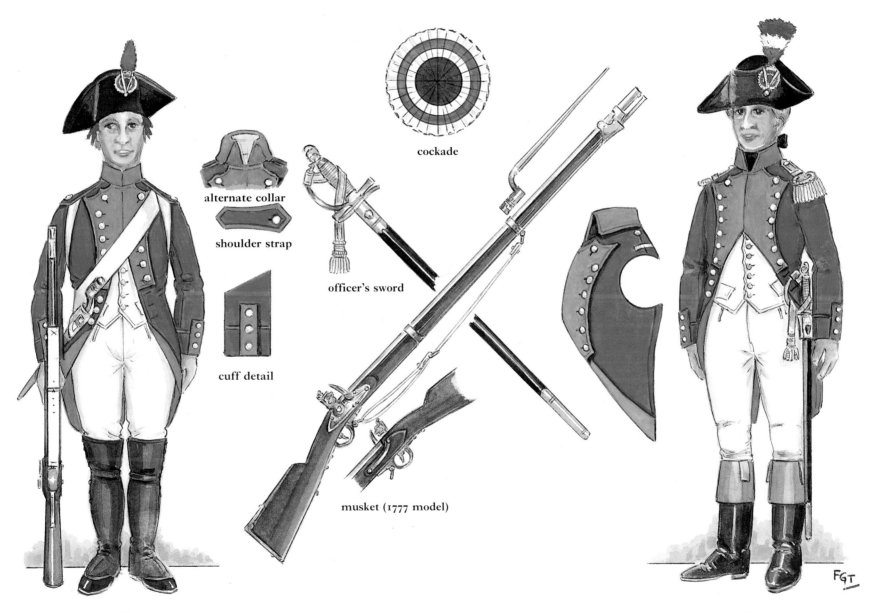

cockade

alternate collar

shoulder strap

officer's sword

cuff detail

musket (1777 model)

fusilier

officer

The basic fighting unit of the Insurgent Army was the **pikeman**. The vast majority wore their ordinary everyday clothes consisting of a grey or off-white shirt, frieze or corduroy knee-breeches and sometimes green or blue garters. Stockings were of various colours, and shoes were black, brown or tan, with a steel or brass buckle on the front. The pikeman illustrated here represents an armed Insurgent of the type in action at Vinegar Hill on 21 June 1798. Had he a coat, he would have discarded it, for the time was mid-summer.

There were **three basic pikes** in use. Some had steel or iron spearheads mounted on a shaft and were best suited for thrusting; in appearance they resembled lances, which cavalry were to carry in later years. Other examples had an edged hook projecting sideways at the base of the blade proper; the hook was used to effect a backward cut, to sever a bridle or unseat a cavalry-man. This type was the most distinctive and is now much associated as a symbol of the period. There were variations to this model; some had a hooked projection at each side of the head (see Plate 3). The final type had an axe-head positioned at the base of the blade on the side opposite the hook. It could be argued that this weapon was technically a halberd but it has always been referred to as a pike in Ireland. Local blacksmiths produced the pike-heads; these in turn were mounted on staves which measured anything between eight and fourteen feet in length. Ash was considered the most suit-able wood for making staves. The pike was to prove itself a formidable weapon time and time again during the Insurrection. Insurgents who were unable to equip themselves with a pike made do with scythes, slanes and pitchforks. Green flags or colours were much in evidence with the Insurgent forces; some measured about two feet square, others were as large as those carried by the King's forces (infantry colours in the King's army during this period often measured in the region of five feet square).

A green **colour** with either a gold or yellow representation of the harp was carried by insurgents in Wicklow, Wexford, Kildare etc. The colour carried by Father Michael Murphy at the battle of Arklow was most likely green but bore a cross and the description LIBERTY OR DEATH. Joseph Holt, the Wicklow leader, had a green colour with his initials JH in yellow on one side, and a harp (most likely yellow) on the other. The colour carried near Kilcullen, Co. Kildare, was also most likely green with the letters IU within a wreath on the centre. At the bottom was the inscription ERIN GO BRA and in the canton a saltire and a harp of the Maid of Erin type; the letters IU may have stood for 'Ireland United'.

While green was the most popular colour with the Insurgent forces, flags of other colours (but not orange) were carried.

PLATE 2
PIKEMAN & INSURGENT FLAGS

1798 flag

Father Michael Murphy's flag

Joseph Holt's flag

Kilcullen flag showing black saltire and Maid of Erin harp

Few **Insurgents** possessed uniforms of any kind, so civilian coats of black or grey with bone, leather or metal buttons were the most common. In many cases, felt 'flower pot' hats were in evidence, often decorated with green or white ribbons, some of which bore the words 'Liberty and Equality' or 'Erin go Braugh' with or without harps according to taste. In addition, green cockades and white feathers made their appearance. Virtually all swords, pistols and muskets that were carried by the Insurgents were captured weapons, apart from fowling pieces which the men of Shelmalier would have used. Black boots, sometimes with tan leather tops, would have been in keeping with leaders' attire. The **flag carried by Thomas Dixon** on Wexford Bridge was black; on one side was a white cross and on the other side a red cross. In addition to these motifs, the flag bore the letters MWS, which apparently stood for Murder Without Sin, although another source states that the letters stood for Marksmen, Wexford, Shelmalier. Anyone within the Insurgent ranks who was fortunate to have a blunderbuss would have used several balls or slugs or suitable metal items when firing – not as accurate as the musket, but particularly useful at close quarters. As a rule this weapon was associated with stage-coaches, town watches and private use; it was not considered a military firearm. It was a short flintlock with a brass barrel and a bell shaped muzzle.

The pike depicted is a variation of the second type which has been described in the commentary on Plate 2.

The **seal of the United Irishmen** included a Maid of Erin harp, a pike and Cap of Liberty, all within a wreath; on the scrolls, the words 'Equality' and 'It is new strung and shall be heard.'

PLATE 3

1798 INSURGENTS

standard-bearer

armed Insurgent

seal of the United Irishmen

FGT

The illustration on the left is based on a contemporary coloured print, drawn from life at Wexford, in the collection of the National Museum of Ireland. Here a genuine attempt has been made by an eyewitness to portray an actual uniform worn by an **Insurgent leader**. The dark-grey or black broad-brimmed hat had a green and white cockade held by a small brass button. The green double-breasted coatee had yellow facings on the lapels, cuffs, turnbacks and shoulderstraps. There was additional yellow braid on the collar and on the black wings which projected from the shoulder straps. The collar had an open front exposing a black stock[1] with a green scarf worn at the base. The most striking feature of the coatee was the lapels, which were worn in this manner to show the facing colour to good effect; otherwise the lapels could be worn buttoned across. The cuffs were pointed. All the buttons on the coatee were brass and were grouped in pairs. A tan leather belt with a steel buckle held a brace of pistols and a captured yeomanry sabre, an important weapon for a leader. Grey breeches with a drop front and black boots completed the uniform.

In the illustration on the right, **Henry Joy McCracken**, the Ulster leader, is depicted wearing a dark green coat which was worn by him at the battle of Antrim on 7 June 1798. This important garment is in the Ulster Museum, Belfast. Now somewhat faded, the collar, lapels, shoulder straps and cuffs are the same colour as the coat. The high collar is of the stand-and-fall variety – a style popular in revolutionary France. All the buttons on the coat are plain brass. On each lapel are ten large buttons grouped in pairs with each button set on a double gold lace buttonhole. The buttons on the cuffs are smaller but are evenly spaced on their respective lace buttonholes. At the back of each cuff are small cloth-covered buttons to enable the cuff to be opened. The pocket flaps are placed on the rear skirts of the coat with each flap having four large buttons at the base of the lace buttonholes and grouped in pairs. On the waist,

between the pocket flaps, are four lace buttonholes, the top pair having large buttons on each seam; and below this arrangement are two large buttons on the seams, partially hidden by the fold on each tail. The turnbacks are white. Under the cream waistcoat, which had a row of silver or pewter buttons, a white shirt frill was worn at the base of the black stock; the frills also appeared on the cuffs. The black waist-belt had a steel buckle. White breeches were worn with black boots with buff tops and straps. His sword, also in the collection of the Ulster Museum, is a straight single-edged weapon with a brass guard and a white bone grip. On the flat end of the pommel is engraved 'Belfast First Volunteer Company'. (The Belfast National Volunteers were raised in January 1793. This unit was influenced by the French Revolution and wore green jackets with yellow facings. It was suppressed by the Government.) The scabbard is black leather with brass mountings, and on the top locket, to which a ring-and-frog button is attached, is the engraving 'ARCHER – DUBLIN'. A white shoulder belt held the sword.

There have been many references to green coats worn by Insurgent leaders. Lord Edward Fitzgerald had a uniform consisting of a green tailcoat with braiding on the front and crimson or rose-coloured cuffs, a cape, a vest and pantaloons. Another of Lord Edward's uniforms was of the hussar type: a jacket, possibly green with overalls reinforced with black leather, a cap of the mirleton type, the lower part green with a crimson wing (see Plate 21). Sadly, none of these references is sufficiently detailed to enable an accurate reconstruction of either uniform. The Wexford governor, Matthew Keogh, had a uniform of green and gold with a cocked hat trimmed with gold lace. Dick Monk wore a green jacket and pantaloons laced with silver, together with a green helmet cap with a white ostrich feather across the top. Some leaders who did not possess green coats wore epaulettes on their civilian attire; others wore green sashes. Matthew Doyle of Arklow wore a red sash.

1 A stock was a form of cravat worn around the neck; at first stocks were of fine leather but later of cloth.

PLATE 4
INSURGENT LEADERS

rear view of
the McCracken coat

Insurgent leader, Wexford

Henry Joy McCracken

PLATE 5: AN OFFICER'S COAT OF THE ANTRIM MILITIA

In 1793, the Irish Militia was raised purely as an infantry[1] force, unlike previous militia arrays which included some cavalry units. No less than 38 different regiments and battalions were formed, and each corps was allocated a numerical prefix in the order of precedence, as settled by the ballot of 8 August 1793.

Their uniforms were almost identical to that of the regular infantry. In the National Museum of Ireland is an **officer's coat** of the 7th or Antrim Regiment of Militia. The coat is in a very good state of preservation and the accompanying illustration is based on this actual garment.

The coat is of scarlet cloth with yellow facings (that is, the colour of the collar, lapels and cuffs). This system of coloured facings served to distinguish one regiment from another. The collar is of the upright type with a fine edge of white piping[2] on the front edges and base. On each side is a loop of yellow thread with a small silver button. All the buttons on the coat, with the exception of those at the back of each cuff, are made of silver and bear a Maid of Erin harp surmounted by a crown and the letters A.M. The lapels are also edged with white piping on three sides. There are ten large buttons on each lapel, set on false yellow thread buttonholes and grouped in pairs. The cuffs have white piping around the top portion and four buttons, grouped in pairs and set on false yellow thread buttonholes. A small cloth-covered button allows the cuff to be opened. Where the white turnbacks meet at the base of the tails there is an embroidered silver wire device with sequins set on a yellow patch of the facing colour. These devices, particularly for officers, varied in design from regiment to regiment. The pockets are placed on the rear skirts, each having four dark red twisted cords, set in pairs and complemented by four buttons which are worn below the flap. On the waist are a further four dark red cords, the top two having a button on each seam. On each shoulder is a silver-lace loop and a small button almost concealed by the collar. These items held the epaulettes in place. This coat is a valuable indication of the pattern worn by officers of the centre (as distinct from light) companies of the various Irish militia corps.

Of the 38 units of militia, yellow was by far the most popular facing colour and was worn by 17 corps; blue was worn by 10 corps; white by four corps and black by four corps, and finally green, which seemed to be the least popular, was worn by three corps.

The following list sets out the coloured facings of each corps, together with their respective numerical prefix.

YELLOW

7 Antrim	23 Carlow	26 Clare	34 North Cork,
29 Fermanagh	11 Galway	14 Kerry	20 Kilkenny
10 Leitrim	13 Limerick City	16 Londonderry	
3 North Mayo	28 Tipperary	33 Waterford[3]	
6 Westmeath[3]	37 Wicklow	38 Wexford[3]	

BLUE

27 Cork City	12 Dublin City	9 North Down	24 South Down
17 Meath	19 King's County	21 Limerick County	
25 Queen's County	15 Longford[4]	2 Tyrone[5]	

WHITE

8 Armagh	32 South Cork	35 Dublin County
30 South Mayo	1 Monaghan	

BLACK

18 Cavan	36 Donegal	4 Kildare	31 Roscommon

GREEN

24 Drogheda,	5 Louth	22 Sligo

On 1 May 1797 the 24th or Drogheda battalion was amalgamated with the 5th Louth, which subsequently became a regiment. The number 24 was given to South Down.

The Meath, Longford and Tyrone units had the prefix 'Royal' added to their titles and naturally wore blue facings when this was used.

---

1 It is interesting to note that early in 1794 orders were issued that 24 men from each regiment be formed into an artillery company. As a rule each corps received two light guns when training had been completed.

2 There is no evidence that white piping was used by other corps; this may have been peculiar to the Antrim Corps.

3 Medals in the collection of the National Museum of Ireland bear the title 'Volunteers' in relation to the Waterford, Westmeath and Wexford corps, all dated 1798.

4 Also referred to as His Royal Highness the Prince of Wales' Regiment of Longford Militia.

5 The title 'Fusiliers' appears on a silver medal in the collection of the National Museum of Ireland, dated 1798.

PLATE 5
AN OFFICER'S COAT OF THE ANTRIM MILITIA

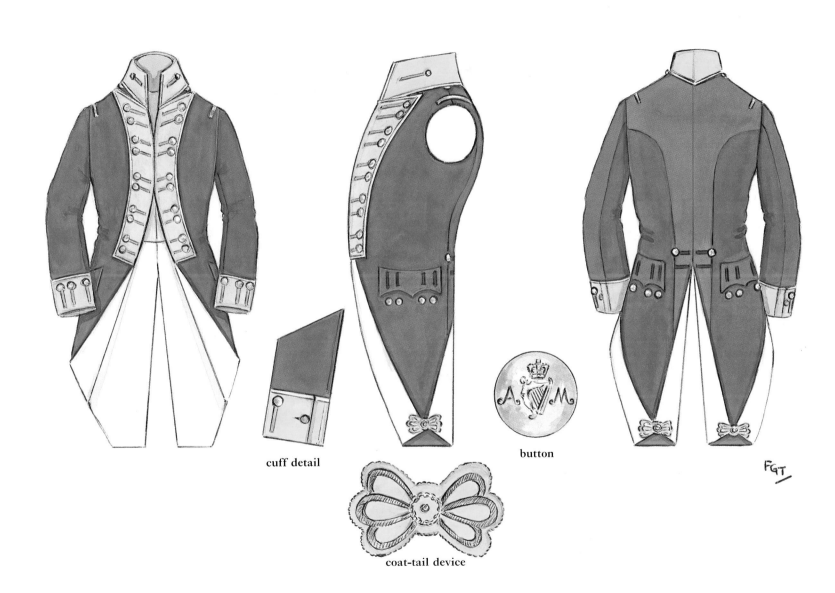

cuff detail

button

coat-tail device

A **junior officer** of the 1st or Monaghan Regiment of Militia This regiment was in action at the battle of Ballynahinch, Co. Down, on 12 June 1798.[1] The black felt three-cornered cocked hat or tricorn had by 1798 almost become a bicorn. On the right point a small gold-wire tassel was worn. Its black cockade was held by a gold-lace loop and a small gold button. The scarlet coat had white facings. All the buttons on the coat were gilt, bearing the numeral 1, with a crown above and the title 'MONAGHAN' below. On each side of the collar was a small button and line of white twisted cord. Each lapel had ten buttons grouped in pairs and set in false buttonholes of white twisted cord. The cuffs carried four buttons and false buttonholes, arranged in pairs. The turnbacks were white, and where they joined at the back tails a small gold-wire embroidered star was placed. The stock was black, and at the collar opening a white shirt frill was shown; likewise frills were often visible below the cuffs. At the base of the collar, a crescent-shaped gilt gorget[2] with white silk rosettes and ribbons was tied to the top buttons of the lapels. This decorative item indicated that the officer was on duty. Many of these gorgets were engraved with the royal arms; others bore the title of the regiment. On the white shoulder-belt, an oval gilt beltplate was worn. As a rule these were engraved with a crown, Maid of Erin harp and the title or number of the corps. At the back of the belt was a white frog which held the sword and scabbard. The back of the coat shows the manner in which the buttons, dark red cord twists and pockets were placed.

Ensigns,[3] lieutenants and captains wore a single epaulette on the right shoulder (in which case the epaulette was gold lace with fine fringes, secured by a gold-lace loop and button). Thicker fringes indicated seniority. **Majors,** lieutenant-colonels and colonels wore epaulettes on both shoulders, with thicker fringes, sometimes in bullion and often a combination of both. If lace was gold for a particular corps, the buttons, beltplate and gorget were likewise. On the other hand, if silver lace was used, the buttons, beltplate and gorget would follow suit.

The waistcoat was white with gilt buttons. The sash, which was also a mark of rank, was of dark red silk net and worn around the waistcoat and under the coat proper; this was knotted on the left side and terminated in long tassels. The white breeches were worn with black gaiters which had small metal or cloth-covered buttons on the sides. The boots were black. The sword was the **1796 pattern** with a gilt guard and hilt; it had two shell guards which afforded better protection than the previous model. A gold lace knot was worn from the guard. The black leather scabbard had gilt mountings.

The uniform worn by a field officer of the 25th or Queen's County Militia is similar in description with the following exceptions and observations. The lace loop, button and tassel on the hat were silver, as were all the buttons on the coat and waistcoat; beltplate and gorget likewise, the latter having blue silk rosettes and ribbons to match the blue facings. Silver epaulettes were worn on both shoulders. On the points of the turnbacks, a silver wire embroidered design was set on a blue patch. In this case the sword was the 1786 spadroon model, with a steel hilt and guard, with a bone grip and a silver-lace sword knot. The black leather scabbard had steel mountings. Field officers were generally mounted, so black leather riding boots and steel spurs were worn. White gloves were worn when required and in general officers' hair was powdered.

---

1 Thomas Robinson's painting of the battle of Ballynahinch, now in Malahide Castle, includes a group of the Monaghan Militia in the centre. Apart from this detail, the artist shows yeomanry cavalry etc, and is one of the most important sources for uniforms of the 1798 period.

2 The origin of the gorget (the French for throat) was a piece of armour worn around the neck. It was retained as a mark of rank until the late seventeenth century. After that it was worn to indicate that the officer was on duty. In 1796 a regulation stated that gorgets were to be gilt for infantry, in theory this would have made silver gorgets non-regulation. Whether this regulation was extended to the Irish Militia, one cannot be certain. Officers who had silver gorgets would no doubt have continued to wear them for the duration.

3 An ensign was originally an officer who carried a flag; the rank was equivalent to a second lieutenant.

PLATE 6
MILITIA OFFICERS

button

1796 sword

1786 sword

junior officer, 1st or Monaghan Militia

senior officer (major), 25th or Queen's County Militia

As a rule, each regiment had, in addition to its centre or battalion company, two flank companies. One of these was the grenadier company; the other was the light company (which will be dealt with in the next plate).

A **grenadier**[1] **of the 4th Kildare Militia** The black felt hat had an edging of white lace, with a black cockade held by a white-lace loop and a small button. Unlike the officers, the men's buttons were pewter, and in this case the button had an eight-pointed rayed star, with the title 'Kildare' on the belt and a shamrock within. Black facings were worn on the collar, shoulder straps, lapels and cuffs on the red[2] coat. The collar had a small button on each side; the ten buttons on each lapel and the four on each cuff were grouped in pairs and worn with false black thread buttonholes. The shoulder straps had a small button on each. Grenadiers wore wings on their shoulders; these were usually the same colour as the tunic but with white lace fringed at the base. A black stock was worn, and at the collar opening a white shirt frill protruded. The turnbacks were white, and on the tails small black heart-shaped devices were worn. The cross belts were white and were held in place by an oval brass belt-plate. These plates usually had the royal cypher or the crowned Maid of Erin harp with the title of the unit engraved on same. Where the cross belts met at the back, one section had a frog to hold the bayonet and scabbard; the other held a black leather ammunition pouch. When skin knapsacks[3] were carried, these necessitated additional white belts which were worn under the shoulder straps and secured by an additional belt worn horizontally across the chest. A row of small buttons was worn on the white waistcoat. The white breeches had small buttons on each side as did the black gaiters which were worn strapped over black shoes. The main weapon was the Brown Bess flintlock musket, of which there were several variations, universally used by the British forces and was the standard weapon of the Irish militia regiments. It had brass mountings and white strap and carried a bayonet whose triangular blade was almost fifteen inches in length. The bayonet scabbard was black with a brass tip.

A **grenadier of the 16th or Londonderry Regiment of Militia** wore a plain black fur cap which carried a plaited white cord, terminating in two tassels on the right side. A group of grenadiers wearing these caps are in evidence in a contemporary print of the battle of New Ross in June 1798 (in the National Library of Ireland). Otherwise the uniform follows that already described for the Kildare Militia except that the facings were yellow. The pewter buttons bear a tower with the title 'Londonderry' above.

The uniform worn by a **private soldier** of the centre or battalion company of the 5th or Louth Regiment of Militia follows the previous descriptions, except that the facing colours were green, thus making the Louth Militia and the Sligo Militia the only two militia units to wear this facing colour in 1798. The buttons of this corps (officer's pattern illustrated) had a crown in the centre with the title 'Louth' above and 'M' below.

---

1 Grenadiers were originally armed with hand grenades. They were considered élite troops and were often selected for their height and physique.

2 Red coats were worn by the other ranks, in contrast to the scarlet of the officers.
3 Goatskin was often used for knapsacks.

PLATE 7
MILITIA REGIMENTS: CENTRE COMPANIES AND GRENADIERS

private, 5th or Louth Militia

grenadier,
16th or
Londonderry
Militia

pewter button

pewter
button

grenadier, 4th or Kildare Militia

silver button (officer's pattern)

FGT/

The light company of a regiment was distinguished by the headdress and the jacket. These troops were expected to move quickly and the shorter coat assisted them in this respect.

A **private soldier** of the light company of the 1st or **Monaghan Regiment**[1] wore a pointed black leather headdress which had a black fur crest and a white metal bugle-horn badge on the front. This symbol had long been associated with light companies because the horn was used to transmit signals in lieu of the drum. The particular headdress worn was one of many patterns associated with light infantry and was possibly a regimental design. The red jacket had white facings on the collar, shoulder straps, lapels and cuffs and along with the pewter buttons and their respective lace buttonholes, were worn in the conventional manner. The turnbacks were white. Woollen wings were worn on the shoulders, and the white shoulder belt with a brass belt plate held the bayonet and scabbard in place. A powder horn with a brown leather strap was worn in addition to a black leather ammunition pouch on the front. White gaiter trousers were worn by this company; they were lightweight and buttoned on the outside of the leg fitting over the shoes.

A **soldier** of the light company of the 2nd or **Royal Tyrone Regiment** wore a headdress consisting of a black round-brimmed hat with a black fur crest and a green plume on the left side (a colour associated with light troops). The Tyrone Regiment had blue facings and laced buttonholes of the bastion pattern but spaced evenly; the shoulder wings resembled those worn by the grenadiers. The rear of the jacket would apply to any regiment, in this case shown with yellow facings and the shoulder strap and wing above. On the small of the back were two buttons with white piping on the lower seams as well as on the centre pleat. The diagonal pockets had four white lace bars and buttons arranged in pairs. In the case of the Tyrone Regiment, bastion-pattern laces would have been the most likely decoration.

In the County Museum, Enniscorthy, Co. Wexford, is an oval brass badge with a crown above. Its inner portion is voided and has a backing of green material – a light infantry colour. The title 'Light Infantry' and 'G.R.' are engraved on the sides; within is a hunting horn and below, the numeral 15.

This was the numerical prefix of the 15th or Longford Militia. It is most likely that badges of this nature were worn on the flaps of ammunition pouches. A pewter button of this corps bears the crest of the Prince of Wales and the motto ICH DIEN, with the title 'Longford Militia' on scrolls above and below.

Attached to each regiment was a band – some large, others small, depending on the strength of the corps. All would have had **drummers**, and the drummers of the Tyrone Regiment were particularly well uniformed.[2] Their black fur caps had plaited white cords with double tassels, and the plate on the front of the cap bore the royal arms and possibly the title of the corps in silver or white metal. The blue facing colours were edged with white lace which had fine red and blue lines. The ten buttons on each lapel set on bastion-pattern buttonholes were evenly spaced. Lace was also worn on the seams of the sleeves as well as five lace 'darts' on the sides. Wings were worn on the shoulders, and the shoulder straps were in the form of white cords. The drum slings and shoulder belt were white, with a sword worn at the back. The shoulder belt had the usual brass plate. The waistcoat, breeches, gaiters and boots were the same as already described. The drums had red and white hoops and on the blue portion was painted an eight-pointed silver rayed star with a gold scroll below.

The illustration of a **drum** of the Leitrim Regiment is based on the original in the National Museum of Ireland. Its most striking feature is the painted centrepiece which takes the form of a shield containing a Maid of Erin harp, surmounted by a crown and flanked by cannon and colours. The crown is gold, decorated with pearls and, within, a crimson cap with an ermine base. On the red shield with a gold border is a gold Maid of Erin harp with white strings. To the left of the crown is a rose with green leaves, and a blue colour containing a Union flag in canton, but devoid of St Patrick's red saltire. Silver finials and gold tassels are common to the other colours and guidon. Below a plain red colour is a ramrod, cannon muzzle and a small red drum. On a white scroll is the title 'Leitrim Regiment' and below the scroll a gold disc bearing an effigy of the sun, with green foliage at each side. (*Continued on page 62.*)

---

1 Details taken from Thomas Robinson's painting.
2 There is a series of watercolours depicting the uniforms of the Tyrone Militia in the Castle Museum, Enniskillen, Co. Fermanagh. These paintings are by Richard Simkin (1850-1926), the most prolific of British military artists. His studies confirm that the Tyrones were exceptionally well uniformed, with decorative laces and other refinements. The details of the drummer were taken from one of Simkin's studies.

PLATE 8

MILITIA REGIMENTS: LIGHT COMPANIES, MUSICIANS, ETC.

private, light company,
Monaghan Militia

drummer,
Royal Tyrone Militia

sergeant,
Royal Meath Militia

brass pouch badge,
light company, Longford Militia

private,
light company,
Royal Tyrone

side-drum, Leitrim Militia

rear view and wing
of light company jacket

pewter
button

The North Cork Militia is frequently referred to during the course of events of the Insurrection, particularly in Co. Wexford. For that reason alone it is important that its uniform be depicted, covering not only the 1798 period but also the immediate years following, to show the various changes to headdress and uniform in general.

The 34th or North Cork Regiment of Militia wore yellow facings, a colour they shared with 16 other militia units. A **junior officer**'s uniform follows the description given for Plate 6 except that the lace, buttons, epaulette, gorget, beltplate and sword knot were silver. The button holes had the usual yellow cord twists and the buttons had the title 'North Cork Militia' around the side and the letters G.R. with a crown above in the centre. The private soldier of the centre company follows the description given on Plate 7. His buttons were of pewter. In the collection of the County Museum, Enniscorthy, Co. Wexford, is another rank's brass beltplate of this regiment. The illustration is based on this example. The plate is oval in shape and bears the title 'North Cork' and the entwined cypher 'GR' with a crown above on the centre.

Towards the end of the eighteenth century, plans were in hand to improve the **dress of the soldier**. The bicorn hat had reached its largest proportions and was replaced by the shako, the first general pattern. This, initially, was leather and cylindrical in shape with a leather peak and was approximately nine inches in height. This pattern of shako was to become known as the 'stove-pipe'. A black cockade was placed at the top with a small button in the centre. Coloured plumes were worn to denote the company the wearer belonged to. White plumes with a red base were worn by the centre company; green plumes were worn by the light company and white by the grenadiers. A large brass plate was worn on the front, this normally carried a universal design which incorporated the royal cypher, the motto 'Honi Soit Qui Mali Pense', trophies of arms and the lion at the base.

A **sergeant** of the North Cork Militia wears the new red single-breasted jacket now devoid of lapels. The yellow facings were worn on the collar, shoulder straps and cuffs. Both collar and shoulder straps were edged with white lace; the latter had white worsted tufts. In place of the lapels, white lace bars were worn in pairs together with the pewter buttons. The lace had a fine blue interwoven line. Chevrons to indicate non-commissioned rank now made their appearance. Sergeants wore three chevrons of regimental lace with each chevron set on a yellow patch of the facing colour (sergeant major, four chevrons; sergeant, three; and corporal, two, respectively). A white shoulder belt with a brass plate held the sword, to which a white sword knot was attached. A crimson sash with a yellow central stripe was worn around the waist and knotted on the left side. Breeches, gaiters, shoes and pike follow previous descriptions. The rear skirts of the jacket had pocket flaps. Each had two sets of lace and buttons. Between the two buttons on the waist seam, a white lace triangle was worn. Sometimes the white turnbacks were edged with lace.

Officers continued to wear the bicorn hat. Their coatees (coats worn closed in front and cut across the waist with skirts behind) were double-breasted and buttoned to the waist, with the front lined in the facing colour. This allowed the coatee to be worn in three different ways: to be worn in plastron fashion by wearing both lapels folded back, as illustrated; with the lapels fastened over to conceal the coloured facings; or with the upper portions of the lapels turned back, thus exposing two yellow triangles. This last method gave a rather dandy effect. Each button had a yellow loop of embroidered thread and the spacings were as for the previous pattern coat. The back skirts of the coatee was almost identical to those illustrated on Plate 6. The epaulette, shoulder belt, beltplate, sash and sword were as previously described. Hessian pattern boots were now in fashion and in many cases were worn with small black tassels.

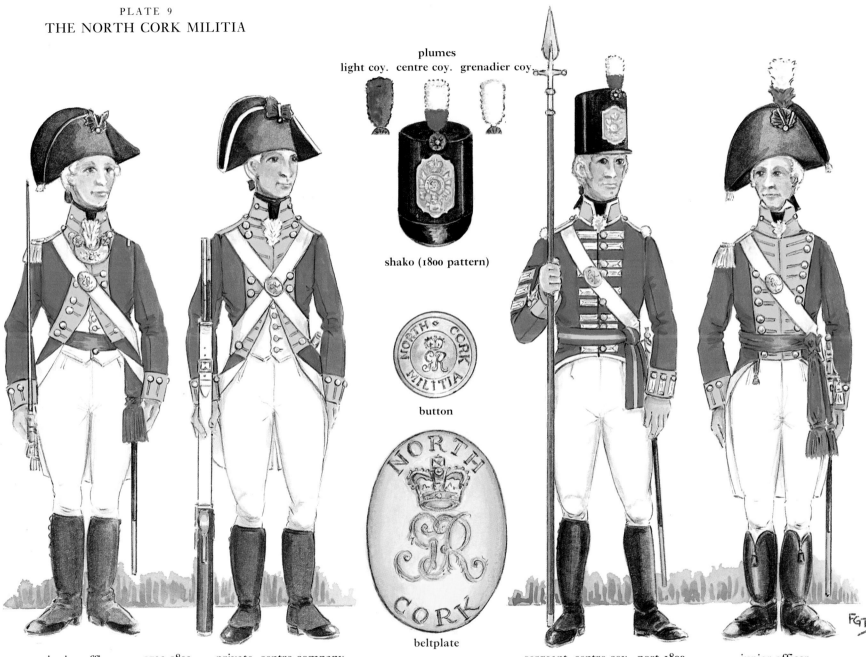

PLATE 9
THE NORTH CORK MILITIA

plumes
light coy. centre coy. grenadier coy.

shako (1800 pattern)

button

beltplate

junior officer   1793-1800   private, centre company   sergeant, centre coy., post-1800   junior officer

In 1796 the government raised and equipped numerous Yeomanry corps, often referred to as District and Volunteer Corps, both horse and foot. These were smaller formations than the militia and were at first confined to their own localities.

In the National Museum of Ireland is a scarlet **officer's jacket and waistcoat** of the Eanmenter Cavalry,[1] a Co. Galway corps commanded by Captain Richard D'Arcy. D'Arcy's name is written in ink under the shoulder wings, so it can be safely assumed that these were his own garments. Both items are in a good state of preservation and are decorated with silver lace and silver buttons, the jacket having dark blue facings. This pattern can be considered the initial type worn by Yeomanry cavalry and can be compared with those worn by a group of Yeomen in Thomas Robinson's painting (see Plate 11).[2] Dark blue as well as scarlet and red were worn by these mounted corps. The blue stand collar has lace on all edges with a fine blue and scarlet edge showing on the top and fronts. Each side has a lace design having a fine scarlet line showing between the laces and within the loops; a small button is placed between these. The lace on the front of the jacket is arranged in plastron fashion. The central lace is a continuation from that on the collar and extends around the bottom of the jacket. There is a fine blue edge to the lace on the front opening, in addition to a row of 16 buttons. On each side of the plastron is a row of 17 buttons. For some reason all the buttons on the jacket, with the exception of those worn on the collar, shoulders, lower cuffs and waistcoat, bear the title 'Eanmenter Cavalry', with the crowned royal cypher in the centre. The buttons worn on these locations are of similar appearance but very slightly smaller, but with 'Auventer Cavalry' engraved. The pockets on each side of the jacket are laced, with a fine blue edging on the top and sides. The blue cuffs are pointed at the front seams and edged with lace with a blue border on the top portions. A lace design, the same as on the collar, is worn on each cuff; and directly above, on the sleeve, this design is repeated but with blue between the lace. The back of the cuff, which can be opened by means of a small button, has laces extending upwards on the seam into three loops, each with blue centres. The rear seams, divided just below the button, exposing a blue ridge within the fold. The buttons placed below the waistline are bordered by four loops each with blue centres and, from the bottom loops, lace extended and terminated in small silver tassels. Blue wings were worn on each shoulder; these had lace around the edges, leaving a blue border. Sewn onto the wings are silver interlaced rings, which to some degree had a practical purpose in protecting the shoulder from sword cuts. From a length of silver bullion cord, fringes of the same type extended. The wings are held to the jacket by small buttons placed on the shoulder nearest the collar, and can be easily removed. The jacket is lined with cream cloth.

The waistcoat (which was lined in red) has a stand collar, laced on the top and front edges and extended down the front and partially to the base, which in turn terminated in oblong designs with pointed ends where a button was placed. The top and front edges of the collar had fine blue and scarlet edges (the opposite to the jacket collar) with blue showing at the outer edge and extending down the centre opening. The front had three equal rows of eight buttons – the pockets were laced on all sides. There was nothing unusual in wearing the jacket unbuttoned, thus exposing the waistcoat.

---

1 Raised as the Eanmenter Cavalry on 31 October 1796. In 1803 their strength was: a captain (Richard D'Arcy), two subalterns, two sergeants, one trumpeter, twenty mounted men and thirty dismounted.

2 At the left of Thomas Robinson's painting of the battle of Ballynahinch are some Yeomanry cavalry wearing red and blue jackets. These jackets carry three rows of buttons which give a plastron effect.

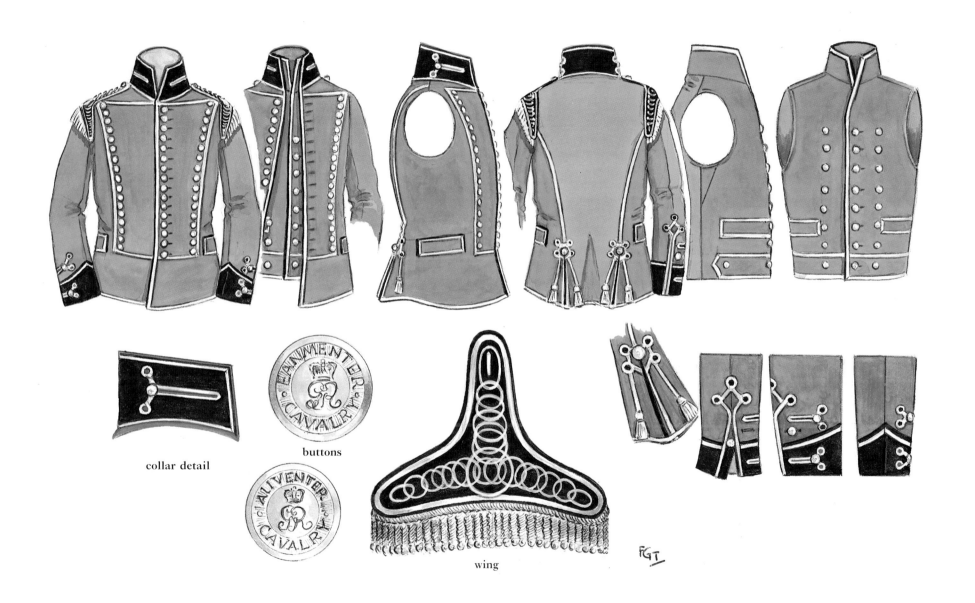

collar detail

buttons

wing

The figures on the left and right are based on details from Thomas Robinson's painting in Malahide Castle.

The black leather helmet with a black fur crest has long been associated with Yeomanry cavalry units in Ireland during this period. It had a pleated turban, in this case red, with fine silver chains affixed at each side. The peak was black leather with silver or white metal edging. At the top of the peak was a silver metal band on which the name of the corps appeared in raised letters. A feather plume, often with a brass tip, was worn on the left side. Plumes were often white, red or a combination of both with red at the base. This headdress was popularly known as the Tarleton helmet (these fur-crested leather helmets were popular with the British Legion in North America during the American Revolution; they were named after Sir Banastre Tarleton, the Legion's commander). At the back of the helmet, a cockade the same colour as the turban was stitched, with tow small silver tassels attached. The dark blue jacket had a red collar, shoulder straps and cuffs, all edged with white lace. A white lace was worn on each side of the collar with a small button, and each shoulder strap had a small button nearest the collar. Blue wings projected from each shoulder strap, both edged white. Three rows of white metal buttons were worn in plastron fashion on the front of the jacket, all extending to the base. The base of the jacket had white piping. Jackets could be worn turnbacked from the waist, thus exposing coloured facings as shown in the figure on the right; a white shoulder belt with silver beltplate, held the sword with two slings. Better equipped units had flintlock carbines which were light cavalry weapons suspended from a clip on an additional shoulder belt. Apart from its 16-inch barrel it resembled the Brown Bess infantry musket. A black leather ammunition pouch, slightly curved, was worn on the front with a white waist belt.

The **sabre** was the 1796 light cavalry pattern.[1] Its wide curved blade made it a weapon more suited for slashing than for thrusting. The grip was wooden and the knot white leather. The scabbard was fitted with two rings. The back of the jacket had lace on the rear skirts and red or coloured turnbacks, edged white. The breeches were white with small cloth-covered buttons at the sides, worn with black leather boots which often had reinforced tops and steel riding spurs.

In the collection of the National Museum of Ireland is a **Tarleton helmet** of the Castlehyde Volunteers.[2] This important example has a black turban with silver chains and a silver band with the title in raised letters. The black rosette has two small silver tassels. On each side of the skull is a silver metal reinforcement.

The **central figure** is based on a study which appears on a glazed jug in the National Museum of Ireland. It depicts a **mounted trooper** of the City of Waterford Cavalry. The Tarleton helmet has a red turban, and the red jacket with a plastron front is similar to that of the Eanmenter Cavalry described on Plate 10. The shoulder wings are of the same type. In addition to the carbine and sabre, a brace of flintlock pistols is accommodated in sheepskin-covered leather holsters placed on each side of the horse's neck. A rolled cape is carried behind the saddle.

---

1 The writer has vivid recollections of witnessing one of these actual weapons being used for purposes it was never intended. On a farm at Drumbenagh, Co. Monaghan, in the 1950s, it was very effective for cutting flax.

2 A County Cork corps. Here the title 'Volunteer' is used; it is usually a term for Yeomanry infantry and not to be confused with the Volunteer movement of 1778-82.

PLATE 11
YEOMANRY CAVALRY: TROOPERS

1796 light cavalry sabre

c.1798

helmet of the Castlehyde Volunteers

c.1796

c.1798

FGT

There was a second and possibly later pattern jacket worn by Yeomanry cavalry, evidence of which appears in Robinson's painting in Malahide Castle,[1] thus confirming that the two patterns were in use at the same time. In the National Museum of Ireland is a good example of an **officer's jacket**, from which these illustrations have been made.

The jacket is dark blue, with pale yellow facings, silver braid and buttons. The yellow collar has a blue border, edged with silver Russia braid (a braid often used to decorate military costume, either gold or silver, of double weave pattern) and small loops, all having blue within. The top and front edges of the collar are yellow. The front of the jacket is very closely braided on both sides, with each braid ending in fine oblong loops with blue centres. From the base of the collar a line of fine braid continues down the front opening edge and continues around the base of the jacket. The arrangement is complemented by an additional fine line which continues from the bottom lace on the front and runs parallel until it takes the form of a trefoil at the back, with each loop having a blue centre. The top six braids on the front extend over the shoulders. There are three rows of plain silver ball buttons and additional buttons on the shoulders at the side of the collar to hold the shoulder cords. On each side of the jacket is a slightly curved double row of braid terminating in a trefoil at each end. Along the back seams are thick rows of lace edged on each side with Russia braid, terminating at the top in leaves and at the bottom in trefoils. At the base of the back are two raised portions covered in yellow and edged in silver. Above the yellow portion of the cuff is a double row of braid with a single loop on the top point and three loops within. The back of the cuff can be opened (there is a small hook and eye for that purpose).

Also in the collection of the National Museum is a Tarleton **helmet of the Ennis Cavalry**, a slightly more elaborate example than the Castlehyde helmet as described in the previous plate. The helmet has a black leather skull and peak, with a black fur crest. The turban is leopardskin and is held at each side by three double rows of gilt chain. The peak has a gilt metal edge, and on the metal band the title 'Ennis Cavalry' appears in raised letters. On each side of the skull is a gilt metal reinforcement. The portion over the ear section is slightly curved and has a brown leather edge. At the back is a crimson rosette from which two small gold wire tassels are suspended. A small gilt button of the Ennis Cavalry has the crowned Maid of Erin harp on the centre. The fact that the helmet fittings and buttons are gilt would indicate the braid on the jackets was gold.

1 On the right section of Thomas Robinson's painting are mounted yeomen wearing this type of jacket. Another valuable source is Robinson's painting of the Inspection of the Belfast Yeomanry being reviewed by the Lord Lieutenant in 1804, from the collection of the Belfast Harbour Commissioners. Both cavalry and infantry are depicted in good detail.

PLATE 12

YEOMANRY CAVALRY: OFFICER'S JACKET, *c.*1798-1803

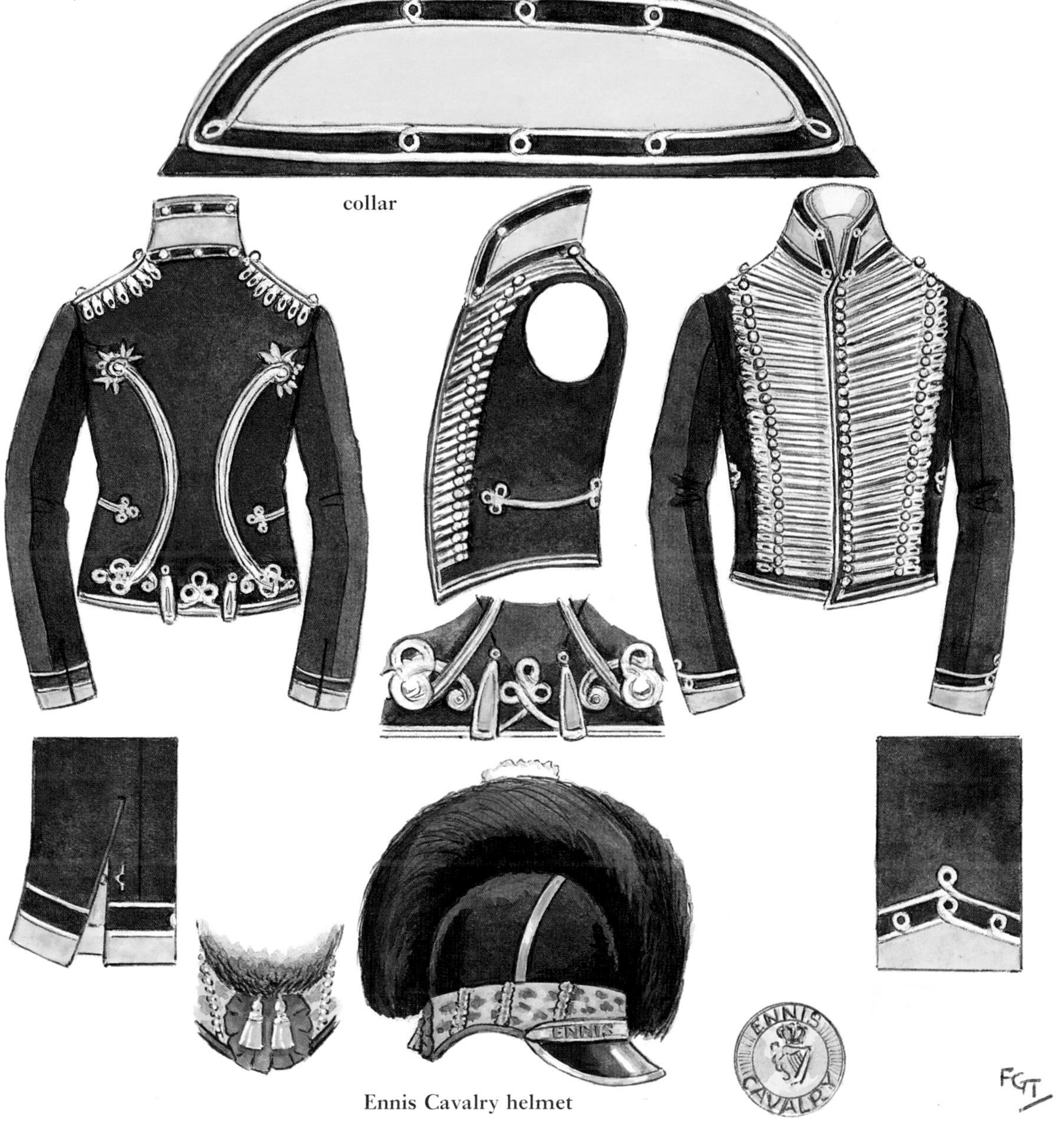
collar
ENNIS
ENNIS
CAVALRY
Ennis Cavalry helmet
FGT

PLATE 13: THE REAY FENCIBLE HIGHLAND REGIMENT OF FOOT, 1794-1802: OFFICERS AND MEN

Between the years 1793 and 1802 numerous Fencible corps were raised in England, Scotland, Wales, Ireland and the Isle of Man. Fencibles were intended to serve in the country in which they were raised for the duration of hostilities; but in this period, many Fencible regiments, particularly Scottish, volunteered to serve in Ireland. The majority were infantry and wore standard infantry uniform, or in the case of Scottish Fencibles, standard Scottish uniforms. The cavalry wore light cavalry uniforms.

One of these corps was the Reay Fencible (Highland) Regiment of Foot, or Reay Fencibles, raised on 24 October 1794 from Lord Reay's estates in Sutherland. The regiment was placed on the establishment on 18 June 1795. Among the locations where the regiment saw action were Naas, Kilcullen, Tara Hill and Hacketstown. In keeping with other highland regiments, the Reay Fencibles wore full highland garb with standard infantry equipment modified to suit their dress.

A **private soldier** of the centre company in marching order The headdress was the highland bonnet and had a diced border of red white and green, with a black leather band at the base of the border. The bonnet was mounted with black bearskin[1] with a droop over the right ear. The top of the bonnet was blue and this was visible under the bearskin. A hackle or plume was worn over the left ear, held by a black cockade with a small regimental pattern button. The plumes were red and white for the centre or battalion company; white for the grenadier company and green for the light company.

The jacket was red with light grey-blue facings. All the buttons on the jacket were pewter with the thistle and star in the centre with the words 'Reay Fencibles'. The lace was white, with a button on each loop; the loops were worn in pairs on the lapels and cuffs and singly on the collar. There was white edging to the shoulder straps. The usual black leather stock with white shirt collar and frill were visible. The crossbelts were buff or white, held in place by an oval brass beltplate which had a crown and a thistle within the star surmounted by the title 'Reay Fencibles' (see Plate 14). At the back, the crossbelts carried a black leather ammunition pouch and a bayonet in a black leather scabbard with a brass tip. An additional white belt was placed horizontally across the chest when the goatskin knapsacks were carried for marching order. This

belt secured the shoulder belts attached to the knapsack. The turnbacks were white and the rear skirts had slashed flaps with four laced loops and buttons on each, arranged in pairs with a white laced triangle at the waist. The white waistcoat had a row of pewter buttons. A belted plaid (breacan-an-fheilidh, kilt and plaid in one) of the MacKay tartan was worn, the top portion of which was fastened to the shoulder strap button at the back. When belted plaids were not worn, a feilebeag (or little kilt) with pleats permanently stitched was worn in lieu. The hose were red and white and were not made like the modern sock but cut out of cloth and sewn at the back. The garters were scarlet with rosettes and ends facing downwards; the tops of the hose were turned down. Low-cut black leather shoes had plain brass buckles fitted. When the sporran was worn by the rank and file for reviews, inspections etc., these were of white goatskin with a straight white metal top, and six black horse hair tassels in metal bells.

A **sergeant** of the centre company wears a similar uniform except that the jacket was scarlet. Epaulettes were worn on both shoulders, the straps blue with white edges and fringes. A worsted crimson sash with a blue central stripe was worn over the left shoulder; and a white belt with a white metal plate (on the right shoulder) held a steel mounted highland broadsword in a black scabbard with a steel tip. The kilt had a sporran of badger skin surmounted by a straight silver rim, and ornamented with six white goat hair tassels mounted in silver metal bells.

An **officer of the centre company** wears a scarlet jacket with silver buttons and belt plate. Epaulettes were worn on both shoulders; these were silver with silver bullion fringes with a gold embroidered thistle on the strap. The gilt gorget had blue rosettes and ribbons. No buttons were worn on the collar laces. A crimson silk sash was worn over the left shoulder and was knotted on the right side. In addition to the broadsword, a silver-mounted dirk with a knife and fork in the sheath was carried on the right side. The sporran was the same as that of the sergeant.

An **officer of the grenadier company** White hackles were worn by the grenadiers, and in some orders of dress, wings with fringes were worn in lieu of the normal silver epaulettes. When on the march or in action, white breeches and black leather Hessian boots were worn in lieu of the kilt and hose. These were also worn by mounted officers,[2] but with spurs.

---

1 In many highland regiments the bonnet was mounted with ostrich feathers. Apparently the Reays adopted the bearskin because it was more economical. The officers would most likely have used ostrich feathers.

2 The mounted officers were the colonel, lieutenant, major and adjutant.

private, centre company   sergeant, centre company   officer, centre company   officer, grenadier company

The Reay Fencibles finally received their first set of colours in October 1796. These important items have survived the years and are in the National Museum of Antiquities in Edinburgh.

The **regimental colour**, the reverse of which is illustrated (left), is light grey blue to match the facings of the regiment. In the top right corner is the first Union flag. In the centre is a circular white satin plaque with a thistle between two leaves, within a rayed saltire (part green), that is, the star of the Order of the Thistle – and surmounted by a crown. Below, on a white gold-edged scroll, are the words 'Reay Fencibles' in gold.

The **King's colour**, the obverse illustrated (right), is in the form of the first Union flag, containing the crosses of St George and St Andrew and used until 1801.[1] In the centre an Adam's shield with the letters G.R. between 'Reay Fencibles', all in yellow embroidery and surrounded by a wreath of thistles and roses. The cords and tassels extending from the brass finial in both cases are gold and crimson mixed. In the centre is an other-ranks oval brass beltplate. This item has been cast with the lettering and ornamentation sunk. The centre has a thistle between two leaves, set on a star of the Order of the Thistle, the uppermost point displaced by a crown with the title 'Reay Fencibles' above. Below the belt plate is a representation of the **MacKay tartan**, which was a lighter shade than that worn at the present time.

---

1 After the Act of Union was passed in 1801 the red saltire of St Patrick was added. Regiments and corps would have received new colours, the old colours laid up or put in safe keeping. Few stands of old colours have survived.

PLATE 14
THE REAY FENCIBLES: COLOURS

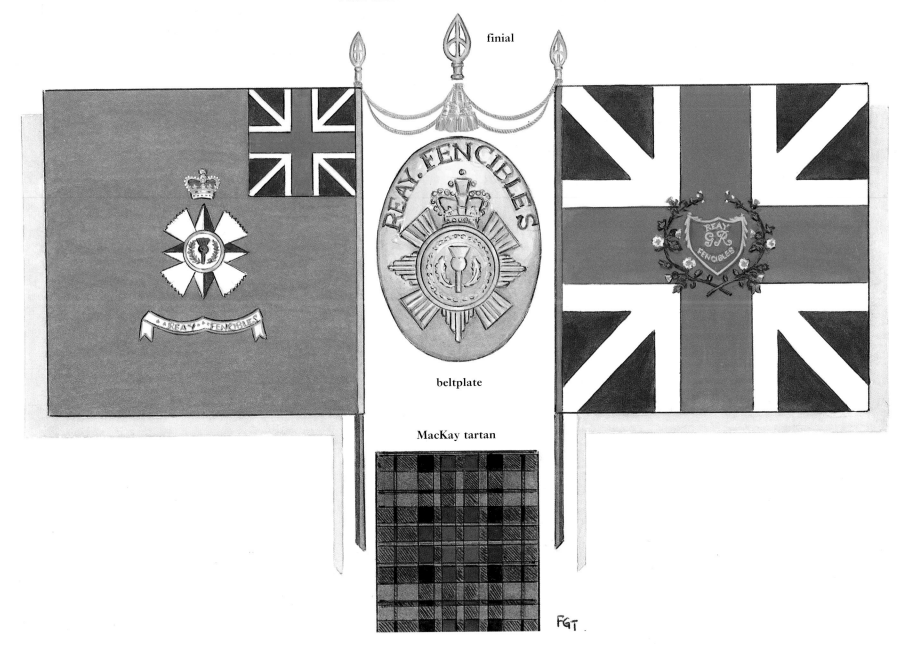

finial

REAY·FENCIBLES

beltplate

MacKay tartan

FGT

In 1756, an Artillery Company of Ireland was formed, which in 1760 became the Royal Irish Regiment of Artillery. During the 1798 period, the regiment first saw action in Ireland at Enniscorthy, where a detachment lost two of their howitzers to the Insurgents. At Tubberneering on 4 June, another detachment lost two six-pounders and a howitzer, and a further six field-pieces to the French 70th Demi-Brigade at Castlebar. The regiment's headquarters was at Chapelizod; as a result of the Act of Union in 1801, the regiment was merged with the Royal Artillery, and during its lifetime it wore the same uniform as the Royal Artillery with some minor exceptions.

An **officer** of the Royal Irish Artillery wore a cocked hat of black felt with a white plume held by a black cockade and a gold lace loop and a small gilt button. The coat, based on a surviving example in the Royal Artillery Institution in Woolwich, is dark blue with scarlet facings, gold lace and gilt buttons – all traditional artillery colours. On each lapel are ten gold lace buttonholes, grouped in pairs, with a single lace on each side of the collar. A scarlet patch shows within each lace, complemented with a gilt button. During the regiment's existence it appears that three patterns of button were used. The button in the centre of the group of three is worn on the coat in question; it is flat, with a sunken shield bearing a crowned Maid of Erin harp with a cannon below. At each side of the crown is a cannon ball. The button on the left has a beaded rim with a shield bearing the Ordnance arms surmounted by a crowned Maid of Erin harp with the title 'Royal Irish Artillery'. The button on the right has a crowned Maid of Erin harp with a cannon below and the title 'Royal Irish Artillery'. I think that the button in the centre would have been the pattern most likely used during the period in question.[1] Gold lace epaulettes, held by small buttons, with gold bullion crescents and fringes, are worn on both shoulders. On the officer's lower sleeves and cuffs the four laces are arranged in chevron fashion, grouped in pairs with a button placed on the centre of each; the top three laces having blue centres, the bottom lace set on the scarlet cuff having a scarlet centre. Also on the cuff is a small cloth-covered button to enable the cuff to be opened. The turnbacks are white with a small scarlet heart-shaped device on each tail. The pocket flaps are three-pointed, with four laces grouped in pairs with a button to complement each loop set below the flap. On the waist between the pocket flaps are four laces, the top two having buttons on each seam; all these laces have blue centres. A further two buttons are placed on each tail seam but partially hidden by the fold. The white waistcoat had a row of small gilt buttons, the breeches likewise but worn on the sides, and around the waist a crimson sash knotted on the left side. The sword had gilt mountings and a gold lace knot, and the black leather scabbard had a gilt tip.

The artillery piece in the centre is a **six-pounder cannon** with a brass barrel mounted on a wooden carriage, painted grey.

A **gunner**'s black felt cocked hat had a white plume held by a black cockade and a yellow lace loop and a small brass button. In addition there were yellow laces on the hat. The dark blue coat had scarlet facings; buttons and laces were evenly spaced and lace was worsted yellow; the cuffs were of a different pattern with four laces worn evenly. The white cross belts carried a priming horn on a red cord, a hammer and prickers for cleaning the vent of the cannon; otherwise the belts carried a white leather ammunition pouch with a brass badge in the form of a crowned Maid of Erin harp set on a red patch and the usual bayonet and scabbard. The turnbacks were white.

Muskets were carried on the march and the essential **ramrod** was a familiar sight with each gun crew.

---

1 A pewter version of this button was noted in 1977 which would indicate that this type was used by other ranks at some period.

PLATE 15
THE ROYAL IRISH ARTILLERY

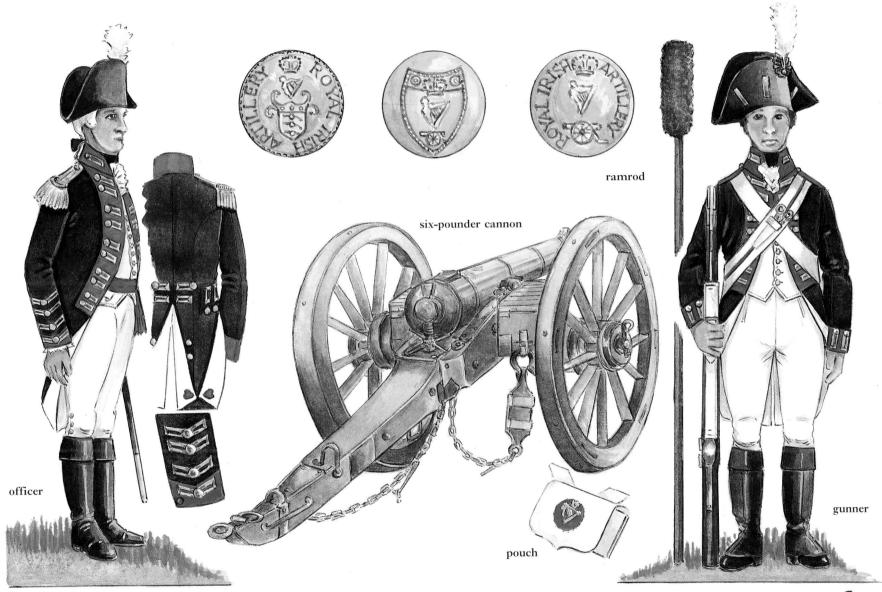

ramrod

six-pounder cannon

officer

pouch

gunner

FGT.

PLATE 16: THE HESSIANS: HOMPESCH MOUNTED RIFLES, 1798-1802

During the war with France, a number of foreign regiments composed of Swiss, Belgians, Dutch, French royalists and Germans offered their service to Britain. One of these regiments, thee Hompesch Mounted Rifles[1] (composed mostly of Germans) became part of the Crown forces. Their appearance was distinctly central European, apart from the cyphers worn on the shabraques (saddlecloths) of all ranks.

This colourful corps was raised by Colonel Ferdinand von Hompesch[2] in January 1798 and was placed on the establishment on 17 April of that year with a strength of 514. The regiment received its mounts in Ireland and it was noted that both horses and men were of good appearance and were permitted to wear moustaches. Some 50 members of this regiment were in action at Vinegar Hill.

The headdress of a **trooper** was in the form of a red cylindrical shako with a white-over-red plume, held by a black cockade and a small brass button in the centre. On the front was a plain brass plate devoid of any engraving. Around the base of the shako was a black pleated turban. The short green jacket had red facings and turnbacks; all buttons brass and the shoulder straps plain. The cuffs were pointed. The lapels took the shape of a half-plastron with buttons worn on each side. The black crossbelts held a black pouch; on one side, from a swivel, hung a carbine, possibly of German manufacture; from the other side, a steel 1796-pattern light cavalry sabre with a black grip and a white knot; the steel scabbard was suspended from two straps. Breeches were red with black leather Hessian-pattern boots and steel spurs. The elegant shabraque or saddlecloth[3] (similar to that shown on the central mounted figure) was green with red Van Dyke edging with a crowned royal cypher in yellow lace. Behind a trooper's saddle a circular green valise[4] with red rings at the ends was placed.

The headdress of an **officer** was a red cylindrical shako with gold lace and cap cords. The plume, taller than the men's, was white over black, below it was a gold cord loop and a green gold-edged cockade with a small gilt button. The top of the shako was wider than the trooper's version. Peaks were detachable. The gold cap cords terminated in flounders[5] and tassels just below the left shoulder. The basic colours of the uniform follows that already described except that the collar, cuffs, plastron, turnbacks and rear sleeve seams had gold lace added. The epaulettes and fringes were gold. All buttons were gilt and the plastron had T-shaped laces on the button holes. The pouch belt was black leather with gold edges and gilt studs. Around the waist a crimson sash and below a red leather swordbelt and slings to hold the sabre and sabretache.[6] All the fittings on the belt and slings were gilt. The clasp was in the shape of an S between two discs. The steel sabre was the 1796 pattern with a gold lace knot. The red breeches had gold lace trefoil knots with black Hessian boots which had gold lace tops and small tassels, fitted with steel box spurs. The shabraque had royal cyphers in gold lace, and black bearskin flounces for the pistol holsters.

1 Also referred to as Chasseurs à cheval, Mounted Riflemen or Dragoons. They were known as Hessians or Hussians, most likely from the state of Hesse; apparently some were recruited from prisons of various European countries and on account of their uniforms and language were often mistaken for French soldiers by the country people.

2 A brother of Baron Charles von Hompesch-Bollheim, who raised other Hompesch units for the British government.

3 Shabraques were usually colourful saddlecloths often decorated with cyphers or regimental devices. Sometimes bordered with lace, in this case with a pattern known as Van Dyke edging, also known as dragon's teeth.

4 A container to carry equipment and utensils.

5 Interlaced plaited knots on the end of cap cords.

6 A leather pouch which hung from the sword belt. These items were often decorated with lace in addition to a regimental crest or cypher.

PLATE 16
THE HESSIANS: THE REGIMENT OF HOMPESCH MOUNTED RIFLES, 1798-1802

officer

method of
suspending
the sabre

officer

FGT

Far removed from the scenes of conflict during the 1798 Rebellion were at least three bodies of men who were part and parcel of the life of Dublin City. To some degree their respective roles were ceremonial; but they are worthy of record, if only for their dress.

Guardsman of the Battle Axe Guard There is some doubt as to when the Battle Axe Guard was actually formed. Henry VIII sent 100 yeomen to escort his lord deputy, the Earl of Surrey, and Elizabeth I sent a similar escort for Sir Henry Sydney in 1575. The earliest royal warrant relating to this body was given by Queen Anne, dated 30 October 1704, stating that a company of battleaxes had been placed on the establishment of Ireland – 'One company of footguards, to be armed with battle-axes, to attend the State and to consist as follows: Colonel and Captain,[1] two Lieutenants, two Sergeants and fifty Yeomen'. It would appear that this Guard corps originated from detachments of the Yeomen of the Guard which were sent over to Ireland to act as escorts for the Sovereign's representative.

The Irish Court Registry of 1797 had this to say: 'These Guards resemble the Company called in England Yeomen of the Guard. They wait in the Castle by turns, with partizans in their hands and long swords by their sides, their habit is of scarlet cloth made in the particular shape in fashion when they were first instituted, with black velvet and gold lace, with badges before and behind, and instead of hats, they wear black velvet caps, the flat crowns and broad horizontal brims, with a band of ribbon in roses.'

The accompanying illustration is based on an engraving depicting members of the Battle Axe Guard on duty at the lying-in-state of the Duke of Rutland in the House of Lords in Dublin in 1787. The description of their dress in the Irish Court Registry is almost identical.

The roses are in red, white and blue. On the breast and back were handsome gold embroidered royal cyphers in the form of a crowned Maid of Erin harp and the letters G.R. The waistbelt and sword frog did not appear to be edged with gold lace. The battleaxes[2] were by this time partizans, a weapon which emerged in the middle of the fourteenth century and eventually became a ceremonial arm with a tapering blade with the shoulders pointing upwards. At the base of the blade was a crowned Maid of Erin harp and the letters G.R. engraved. A large dark red and gold tassel was placed at the base of the brass socket below the blade. The sword had a brass grip and guard with a black scabbard and a brass tip. The hose were white with black shoes and brass buckles. It is not possible to describe the officers dress during this period. In the late 1820s they wore the coatee. The guards carried out their duties at Dublin Castle, attending the Lord Lieutenant. The Battle Axe landing in the castle is named after them. The Battle Axe Guards were disbanded in 1833.

Pensioner of the Royal Hospital, Kilmainham Four years after the Duke of Ormonde laid the foundation stone to the Royal Hospital, Kilmainham on 29 April 1680, the first pensioners took up residence in this retirement home for old soldiers. It was to follow in the same tradition as Les Invalides in Paris. Its British counterpart, the Royal Hospital, Chelsea, was completed two years later. In 1928 this venerable institution closed its doors and the remaining pensioners were transferred to Chelsea. The uniforms worn by the Kilmainham pensioners closely resembled those of their Chelsea counterparts. The black cocked hat had gold-lace edging with a distinctive black Hanoverian cockade,[3] held by a gold-lace loop and a small brass button. The long scarlet coat had a blue collar, cuffs and pocket flaps, the cuffs and flaps edged with gold lace. There was a row of eight brass buttons on the front and each buttonhole had a fine loop of dark-red thread. At the collar opening was a white frill and a small button on each side. Large buttons were worn on the tops of the cuffs and below the pocket flaps on the coat. The hose were black with black shoes and brass buckles. On other occasions black gaiters would have been worn.

City Battle Axe[4] Although, technically not a military body, the Lord Mayor of Dublin's household included at least ten halbardiers titled the 'City Battle Axes'. Their brown flat-crowned hats (intended to resemble the mayoral cap of maintenence) had blue and white (*continued on page 62*)

---

1 The original title of the officer commanding was 'Captain of the Company of Foot Guards armed with Battle Axes'. His rank was the equivalent to a colonel of a regiment of foot.

2 The Battle Axe Guards were the successors to a force of government gallowglasses who acted as a guard to the lord deputy. This body of men, who disappeared early in the seventeenth century, were armed with conventional battle axes.

3 Black cockades were introduced by George I, this particular type was made of leather and was known as the Hanoverian cockade.

4 A contemporary painting by P.J. Haverty (1794-1864) in the collection of the Bank of Ireland records the visit of George IV in 1821. Just behind the Lord Mayor's coach, an officer of this body is in evidence, although somewhat indistinct; he carries a halberd and a sword.

PLATE 17
THE NON-COMBATANTS

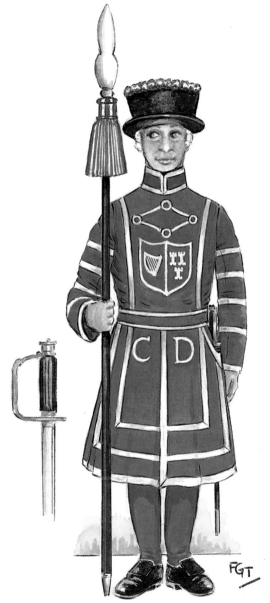

guardsman of the Battle Axe Guard

pensioner of the Royal Hospital, Kilmainham

City Battle Axe

When this regiment was raised in 1715, it was known as Wynne's Dragoons, named after its colonel; from 1751 it was called the 9th Dragoons and subsequently the 9th Light Dragoons when the regiment was converted to light cavalry in 1783. The 9th had been quartered in Ireland for some considerable time prior to 1788 and during the Insurrection saw action at Vinegar Hill. From 1784 their general appearance differed considerably. As their title implies, the men were supposed to be light and small, their horses likewise, and their headdress, clothing and weapons more compact and less cumbersome than that used by heavy cavalry. The figures are based on Richard Simkin's studies of the uniforms of 1784.

Trooper The Tarleton helmet was now the headdress for light dragoons and in this case, had a buff-coloured turban, fastened with chains and a white feather plume (in 1794 a white-over-red-feather plume was authorised; Simkin shows it as white). The blue sleeveless jacket was in fact a shell which was worn over a sleeved waistcoat or underjacket. This shell had wings piped white, to give a neat appearance where the sleeves of the waistcoat emerged, often giving the impression that the sleeves belonged to the shell. In 1796, the shell and underjacket were replaced by a jacket proper, but it is not certain that the regiment actually received these during or prior to the 1798

period. The shell had buff facings on the collar, shoulder straps, cuffs and turnbacks; all these areas had white piping. The decorative loopings across the front of the shell were white; the rear skirts had white lace lines with trefoils at the top and tassels at the bottoms in addition to a central white lace edging on the vent. The turnbacks had a blue heart-shaped device on each point. All the buttons would have been pewter with the motif 'IX' above 'Ds'. The backs of the cuffs could be opened. The crossbelts were buff with a brass buckle and held a pouch with a carbine swivel attachment as well as the slings for the 1796 sabre and bayonet frog. The sword knot had a white tassel. Breeches were buff leather with small covered buttons. Black leather boots with cuffed tops and steel spurs; and, for dismounted duties, black gaiters were worn in lieu. A detail shows the **practical purpose of the sword knot**; this allowed the pistol or carbine to be fired while retaining the sword close to hand.

The **uniform worn by the officers** follows the same description with the following exceptions. All lace and buttons were silver. The epaulettes, worn on both shoulders, had silver lace and fringes with blue showing between the two loops. The swordbelt had a silver or white metal buckle and the buff sword knot had a gold tassel.

PLATE 18

THE 9TH LIGHT DRAGOONS

trooper

the practical use
for the sword knot

rear view of jacket and cuff

button

officer

FGT

This heavy cavalry regiment can trace its lineage to the first of two regiments of dragoons which formed part of the Inniskilling forces in the service of William of Orange. During these early years it was known by the colonel's name. Between the years 1704 and 1751, the regiment was titled the Royal Dragoons of Ireland and from 1751 was known as the 5th (Royal Irish) Dragoons. After the battle of New Ross, the 5th enlisted a number of new recruits who proved to be disguised insurgents. A plot to massacre the officers and older soldiers was laid, but the timely discovery of this plot averted disaster. As a result the regiment was disbanded on 15 April 1799 at Chatham, and the officers and men transferred to other corps.[1] The accompanying illustrations are based on drawings by Richard Caton Woodville (1856-1927) and from an 1800 print in the British Military Library.[2]

The headdress of a **trooper** was a black plain cocked hat which had now reached its largest dimension, with small white tassels at each end. A white feather plume was set above a black cockade which was held by a metal scale loop. The single-breasted red jacket had a row of buttons with five double loops of white lace on each side. The buttons were pewter and were engraved with the letters 'Vth R I Ds' with a crowned Maid of Erin harp in the centre. The facings were dark blue on the collar, cuffs, shoulder straps and turnbacks, all with piping or lace; both collar and cuffs had lace loops, the latter usually obscured by white gauntlets. Red wings were worn on the shoulders and these had white lace. Over the left shoulder, a white belt was worn to which was fitted a metal swivel to hold the carbine and a black leather pouch which held 30 rounds. In addition, a white waist belt with a brass rectangular clasp and slings to hold a **1796 heavy cavalry sword** and a bayonet frog. The sword had a straight 35-inch blade with the base of the guard in the shape of a pierced pear-shaped disc; its grip was dark brown and the sword knot of white leather. When the carbine was not suspended from the swivel, it was carried strapped to the horse with the muzzle held in a leather cup. The blade of the bayonet was 15 inches long and the pistol holsters were covered by black bearskin flounces. The breeches were white with high black boots which had hollow back portions and steel spurs. In 1796, a brown leather regulation saddle was introduced, but the bridle, reins and other straps were black. At the back of the saddle, a rolled red cloak with the lining outwards was affixed.

The **officer's uniform** follows the same description except that the cloth was scarlet and the scale loop, tassels, laces and buttons were silver. The wings on the shoulders had silver fringes. A crimson sash was worn around the waist knotted on the right side. The sword was the 1796 officers' pattern with a gilt guard, and a gold-lace knot with a crimson line and tassel.

---

1 It was not until 1858 that Queen Victoria directed the revival of the regiment as the 5th (Royal Irish) Lancers.

2 By the time this print was published, the regiment was disbanded. It also depicts the feather plume with a red base.

PLATE 19
THE 5TH ROYAL IRISH DRAGOONS

button

hat

heavy-pattern
cavalry sword
(other ranks)

cuff detail

heavy-pattern
sword (officer's)

trooper

officer

Towards the end of 1797 it was decided to increase the forces in North America. An Act was passed to add a fifth battalion to the 60th (Royal American) Regiment. Lt-Col. Baron de Rottenburg of Hompesch's Corps was appointed colonel and the battalion was formed at Cowes, Isle of Wight, to serve in America only; however, as it happened, the 5th served in Ireland during this period. This corps was the first green-coated rifle battalion in the Army, bearing in mind that the other four battalions of the 60th Regiment were red-coated. The personnel were all foreigners, mostly Germans, and were permitted to wear moustaches. In addition they were equipped with rifles instead of muskets.

Rifleman, 5th Battalion, 60th Regiment Not only was this corps of infantry the first to wear green, it was the first to wear the shako headdress. This model was black leather but slightly wider at the top than the 1800-pattern shako. Around the top was a green band and a green plume above a red cockade, with a small pewter button in the centre. Just below the cockade was a silver bugle-horn.[1]

The dark green jacket had red facings and a row of pewter buttons. The black stock was often complemented with a frill. Both piping on the front of the jacket and turnbacks were red; the green shoulder straps and wings likewise. The black cross belts were held in place by an oval brass beltplate bearing the numeral 60. Green cords with prickers were looped around this area. At the back, attached to these belts was a black ammunition pouch and a frog to hold the black scabbard with a brass tip. Initially, bayonets could not be fixed to many of the rifles, so short swords were issued in lieu. In the early stages, various types of rifle were in use; some of these would have been continental but in due course the famous Baker rifle was issued together with a sword-bayonet which had a straight blade and a bayonet fitting. The blue-grey breeches had red piping on the sides and red bastion pattern laces on the front. Black gaiters, with red top edges and pewter buttons on the sides, were worn over black shoes.

Officer, 5th Battalion, 60th Regiment Officers of this battalion also wore dark green but of a style completely different to that of the men, resembling a light cavalry uniform. The headdress was the Tarleton helmet with a black peak and skull and a black fur crest. On the left side a green feather plume with a red cockade and a small silver button. The green turban had silver chains, and the peak a silver rim. The collar and cuffs, which were pointed, were decorated with silver lace. On the front were black laces and three rows of silver buttons. The opening and bottom edges of the jacket were also black. The green shoulder straps and wings were edged with scarlet and within both were interlaced silver rings. The wings had silver fringes and a small silver button was placed at the neck end of each strap. Across the chest a black leather shoulder belt was worn; this had a silver Maltese cross on the centre and a silver ornamental boss, whistle (used to call the men to perform various operations) and chains. A pouch, most likely black, would have been worn at the back of this belt attached by silver rings. A crimson barrelled sash with cords and tassels was worn around the waist. Just below the sash was a black sword belt and slings, with a silver snake clasp and fittings. The sword had a curved blade with a gilt guard with a black sword knot, and black leather scabbard with gilt mountings. The dark green breeches had black lace designs terminating in knots (plain blue grey trousers without piping were worn with undress). The black boots were of the Hessian pattern with small tassels.

Marquis Cornwallis, Charles Mann, first Marquis and second Earl, Viceroy and Commander in Chief in Ireland, 1798-1801 The scarlet undress coat had blue facings and gilt buttons arranged in groups of three. Here the garment is shown buttoned across, but it was often worn open, showing the lapels to full effect and the white waistcoat with small gilt buttons. The gold fringed epaulettes had small scarlet patches showing within the loops at each end. A gilt button at the collar end held each epaulette in place. The familiar black stock was worn around the neck with a frill just below. One button was placed on the blue portion of the cuff and, below, shirt frills were visible. The black felt cocked hat had a black cockade with a gold-lace loop and button. White breeches were worn with black boots which had cuffed tops and gilt spurs. The straight sword, suspended from white leather slings, had a gold-lace knot and a black leather scabbard with gilt mountings. On the left breast, the silver eight-pointed star of the Order of the Garter (most portraits depict Cornwallis wearing the deep blue ribbon (*continued on page 62*)

---

1 The badge symbolised the bugle-horn which was used to transmit signals in the same manner as for light infantry corps.

PLATE 20
REGULARS

rifleman, 5th Battalion,
6oth Regiment

officer, 5th Battalion,
6oth Regiment

Marquis Cornwallis, Viceroy

officer, 6th Regiment of Foot

officer's button,
6th Regiment

The small French expeditionary force under the command of **General Joseph Amable Humbert** which landed at Killala Bay on Thursday 23 August 1798 was primarily an infantry force composed of the 70th Demi-Brigade. This force did, however, include artillerymen and some cavalry from the 3rd Hussars.

An **artillery gunner** wore a black cocked hat had a red plume worn over the brim. The dark blue coat with a stand collar had red-fringed epaulettes, red turnbacks and cuffs and piping on the collar and lapels. Dark blue grenades were worn on the base of each turnback. The blue cuff patches were three-pointed and edged red. All the buttons on the coat and waistcoat were yellow metal. Both waistcoat and breeches were blue. The black gaiters, worn over black shoes, had a row of small cloth covered buttons. All belts and the musket sling were white, and where the cross belts met at the back a black ammunition pouch and a small sword with a red knot were carried. A skin knapsack was attached to the shoulder belts. The musket would have been the 1777 pattern.

Trooper, 3rd Hussars The 3rd Hussars were raised by and named after Count Esterhazy in 1764. In 1791 they were renamed 3ᵉᵐᵉ Régiment de Hussards. Their uniform was a distinctive silver grey. The tall dark-grey felt merliton headdress had black leather edging on the top and base and a long black and white wing terminating in a white tassel, which was wrapped around its body. A red feather plume was secured at the base by a circular cockade bearing the arms of the Republic – blue, white and red. Red cords terminated in red flounders and tassels.

The silver grey dolman (a tight fitting jacket worn by light cavalry on the continent, particularly Hussars) had an open stand collar with a black stock. The collar, shoulder straps, front and bottom edges were laced with red, the front having three rows of white metal buttons. The pelisse was also silver grey and was usually worn on the left shoulder; it had black fur edges, and red braid with white metal buttons. The red cuffs were pointed and the red-and-white barrel sash had red cords and tassels. Below the sash a white sword-belt and slings were worn to hold the sabretache[1] and sabre. The snake clasp

and fittings were white metal. The sabre had a brass guard with a white knot, and a black scabbard with brass mountings. Both the shoulder belt and carbine belt were white, the former having a black pouch and the latter having a 1786 musketoon (light musket) attached to a swivel.

The grey overalls had black leather reinforcements on the inside leg and bottoms and the outer seams had a black lace stripe and white metal buttons.

General Joseph Humbert There was a certain degree of individual taste exercised by generals of the new Republic, and it was more than likely that General Humbert had several uniforms. In this respect, the more conventional generals' uniform consisting of a cocked hat and blue coat comes to mind. The accompanying illustration of Humbert is based on an oil painting of the period depicting him wearing a uniform reputedly worn at Castlebar. The uniform is very much 'a la Hussar', a style that was to follow in many armies even though the uniform did not belong to an official Hussar corps.

The red merliton had a red wing edged gold which was wrapped completely around the headdress. Both top and base had black leather edgings. The light blue plume was fitted to the top edge and the gold cords terminated in tassels; at the side, a tricolour cockade was worn.

The dolman was light blue with gold lace on the collar and front edge; across the front were gold laces with small dome-shaped gold buttons. A crimson barrel sash was worn around the waist. A red pelisse with white fur edges and lining was worn over the dolman. All the braid, lacing and buttons on the pelisse were gold. A crimson shoulder belt, edged and decorated with gold lace was worn over the pelisse,[2] this would have held a pouch suitably decorated at the back. The light blue breeches had a gold lace stripe, edged with fine braid, on each side; the front portions decorated with a gold lace design. The black leather boots had gold lace tops and tassels. The sword belt and slings were crimson leather, all edged gold with gold buckles, rings and fittings. The sabre is of the French light cavalry pattern, with a black grip, gilt guard and gold knot; its ornate gilt scabbard having a variety of designs. The handsome sabretache had a crimson front which was decorated with gold braid designs; the centre panel with a gold lictor's fasces. (*Continued on page 62.*)

---

1 The decoration on the front of the sabretache usually comprised republican symbols and the regimental number.

2 In their original form these were said to have been wolfskin worn by the early Hungarian hussars; later the pelisse became fur-lined and duly ornamented and usually worn on the left shoulder when not worn as an over-jacket.

PLATE 21
THE FRENCH (I)

detail of
coat-tail

artillery gunner   trooper, 3rd Hussars   General Joseph Humbert   Theobald Wolfe Tone

FGT

The vanguard of General Humbert's force was the 70th Demi-Brigade. In 1793, a Republican Army was established and the title of regiment with regard to the infantry of the line was abolished. In its place the Demi-Brigade was created. This was a formation consisting of three battalions, one of which was regular and the other two composed of new volunteers. Each battalion had its own colour.

The headdress of a **fusilier** was a black felt bicorn with a lemon yellow pompom worn above a tricolour cockade which was held by an orange lace loop and a small yellow metal button. Hair was often worn long in contrast to the powdered wigs of the former Royal Army. The blue coat had already been worn by the National Guard and was made the standard issue for the Demi-Brigades, thus replacing the variety of dress which had passed for uniform. This coat had a red collar and cuffs both piped white and red piping on the shoulder straps, lapels and turnbacks. All the buttons on the coat and waistcoat were yellow metal.

The blue shoulder straps had a small button and were pointed at both ends. The lapels were white and each had six buttons at the edge and a single button at the top point. On the right edge of the coat below the lapel were a further three buttons. Each cuff had three buttons which allowed the cuffs to be opened, and just above the cuff on the lower sleeve was a line of red piping. The rear skirts of the coat had two three-pointed slashes, piped red with three buttons on each, and a single button above each on the seam. On the base of each white turnback was a coloured cloth device. During the *ancien régime* a fleur-de-lis, a symbol closely associated with the French monarchy, was worn by troops of the centre companies. During the early days of the Republic it was possible that no device was worn.[1] Grenadiers wore red grenades, as illustrated and voltigeurs a green bugle horn. In addition grenadiers wore red fringed epaulettes and were also supposed to wear bearskin caps, but owing to scarcity of material this was not always possible, although, to some degree, fur caps were worn after the Revolution. Both the waistcoat and breeches were white and black gaiters with buttons on the sides; these were worn over black shoes. A single white shoulder belt would have had a black leather ammunition pouch attached at the rear but also carried the bayonet and scabbard on the right side. The white straps worn over the shoulders held a skin knapsack. The 1777 pattern musket had a white sling.

The **colour** of what appears to be that of the 2nd Battalion of the 70th Demi-Brigade was captured by Private Toole of the Armagh Militia when his regiment was in action at the battle of Ballinamuck, Co. Longford. This colour, now in the care of the Armagh Public (Robinson) Library, has some holes, possibly caused by gunfire or age or a combination of both. Colours of Demi-Brigades varied considerably with the intention of incorporating the national colours of blue, white and red in some form within the basic field. This particular example was the 1794 style and compares closely with a similar colour carried by the 2nd Battalion, 57th Demi-Brigade. The basic colour was white with a representation of a tricolour canton in the top left corner nearest the pole, where blue above white above red were placed. The red panels below the canton and on the sides have not survived, either due to fading or becomming detached during attempts to preserve the colour in times past. In the centre field is a bundle of brown lictors' rods with steel axeheads at each side, the rods bound by green foliate and surrounded with a green wreath. Above is a red Phrygian cap with gold chin pieces and a green wreath. The title 'RÉPUBLIQUE FRANÇAISE' and the numerals are gold. Just beside the numeral 2 is a void which may well have had 'EME' indicating 2nd Battalion. Tricolour ribbons and tassels were often suspended from the base of the brass finial. Sometimes the poles were of natural wooden colours, but in some cases they were painted blue or in tricolour colours.

The colours of the **officers' uniform** closely followed that of the men's with the following exceptions. The large felt bicorn hat with a red over white pompom and a tricolour cockade held by a gold lace loop and a small gold button. All buttons on the coat and waistcoat were gold. The epaulettes were gold, with fringes worn on the left shoulder only.[2] At the base of the collar, a gilt gorget[3] suitably crested was tied with a fine gold cord. Waistcoats were either white or light buff and the breeches, white, with small buttons on the sides. The black leather boots had buff leather tops and straps. The sword had a brass guard with a leather knot, a black scabbard with brass mountings was worn from a white leather frog.

---

1 In due course the letter N with a crown above was used by fusiliers.
2 An epaulettes without fringes was known as a contre-épaulette.

3 The gorget or 'Hasse-Col' during the republican period was usually crested in silver with symbols like the cap of liberty, lictors' rods and trophies of arms.

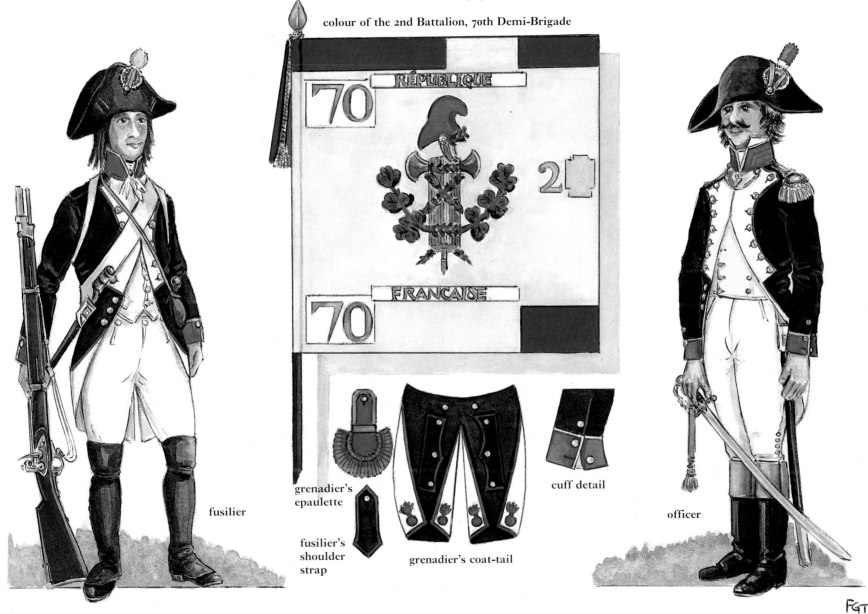

PLATE 22
THE FRENCH (II)

colour of the 2nd Battalion, 70th Demi-Brigade

RÉPUBLIQUE

70

2

FRANÇAISE

70

fusilier

grenadier's
epaulette

fusilier's
shoulder
strap

grenadier's coat-tail

cuff detail

officer

FGT

Robert Emmet's attempted rising in July 1803 produced little change in the appearance of the rank and file.

Armed Insurgent Like their predecessors, civilian clothes were worn, and they armed themselves with anything they could lay their hands on. The more fortunate had muskets or pistols but some had **blunderbusses** fitted with spring bayonets.

Robert Emmet's flag A flag was found in the building where Emmet had gathered material for his insurrection. This was a green flag with a yellow harp with a figure of a winged maiden. Behind the harp was a spear or pike 'crowned' with a scarlet Phrygian cap of liberty. On a yellow scroll beneath the harp were the words 'Erin Go Bragh'.

Robert Emmet When Robert Emmet led his rising he wore a dark green coatee laced with gold and with gold epaulettes. In the collection of the National Library of Ireland is a detailed colour print on which the accompanying illustration is based. The dark-green double-breasted coatee had crimson lapels[1] which were decorated with gold lace loops terminating in trefoils; the longer loops had small gold buttons. The black stock was complemented by a white frilled shirt and cravat. The gold-fringed epaulettes appear to have two small objects, possibly stars, to represent rank insignia. On the cuffs the gold lace was relieved by two small buttons. The front edge of the coatee had crimson piping. Two rows of gold buttons were worn on the front, and around the waist was a gold sash or belt with sword slings. The sword had a gilt guard and a black grip with a gold lace knot, and the black scabbard had gilt mountings. A gilt white-handled stiletto was attached to the belt. Off-white or buckskin breeches were worn with black Hessian-pattern leather boots. The black felt cocked hat had a white feather. A crimson cloak with a brown fur collar was draped over his shoulders. The collar was held by gold cords terminating in tassels.

Other insurgent leaders had uniforms similar to Emmet's but with one epaulette. In addition Quigley's hat had a white feather, and Stafford's a green feather. Emmet sent a green coat with large epaulettes to Michael Dwyer. This indicates that a serious attempt was made to show rank insignia.

---

1 Some prints depict Robert Emmet's coat with white or buff facings. The Irish National Foresters in later years adopted this uniform. They can still be seen in Wexford and other towns on St Patrick's Day.

PLATE 23
ROBERT EMMET'S INSURRECTION, 1803

ERIN GO BRAGH

Robert Emmet's flag

blunderbuss with spring bayonet

armed Insurgent

Robert Emmet

The Bank of Ireland was authorised to form a corps of Yeomanry in 1797; this was a supplementary unit, serving without pay. The corps was officered by those bank directors who held military commissions, and was titled the 'Bank Infantry'. In 1800 the coat was replaced by the coatee and the cocked hat gave way to the shako. These changes affected the Yeoman infantry corps as well as the regulars and the militia.

Captain, Bank Infantry The illustration on the left is based on a painting of a captain of the Bank Infantry by Robert Gibbs[1] in the collection of the Dublin Civic Museum. The headdress is a type of bicorn mostly associated with officers of dragoons and dragoon guards and intended for wear at levées and other social functions.[2] It was of black felt or beaver with a white-over-scarlet feather plume and an elaborate gold embroidered star on the right side and gold tassels at each point. The scarlet jacket with its dark blue collar and cuffs is very similar to the style worn by dragoons of the same period. The front is decorated with five loops of gold lace worn in pairs with gilt buttons; the front edges of the jacket are edged with gold lace and the turnbacks likewise. A fine scarlet line is visible on each lace loop. The cuffs form gold laced loops, grouped in pairs, with gilt buttons on the centre of each, the loop on the blue portion of the cuff having a fine blue line. There is a fine line of white piping around the cuff and on the top and front edges of the collar. The collar laces have blue lines within and at the base of the black stock a white frill shows. The shoulder wings are made of gilt interlaced rings and gold lace edging set on dark blue patches edged with white piping. Around the waist is a crimson sash knotted on the left side. The gold lace sword belt and slings to hold the sword and sabretache had redleather backing; the snake clasp, fittings and rings are gilt. The 1796 pattern sword had either a pearl or silver-wire grip with a gilt guard and gold lace knot; its black scabbard had gilt mountings. Only the back of the black leather sabretache can be seen in the portrait, so it is not possible to say what motif or crest decorated the front. The gloves and breeches were white, and the black

Hessian boots had gilt box spurs which would indicate that an officer of his rank was mounted.

The uniforms of the men would have probably resembled those of the College Infantry but in the collection of the Bank of Ireland is a rectangular brass beltplate with a convex dome in the centre bearing the entwined letters B.I. surmounted by a crown.[3]

The figure in the centre represents an early Dublin 'policeman' or **parish constable**, wearing a 'flower pot' hat and caped overcoat. These officers were part of the life of the city, and some of them were issued with swords, pistols and, no doubt, the odd blunderbuss. With the advent of uniformed police some ten years later, these familiar figures began to disappear.

A Yeomanry infantry corps titled the 'College Infantry' was raised on 31 October 1796 in Trinity College, Dublin. There were four companies and by 1803 numbered 300 all ranks.

Private, College Infantry The headdress was the black leather shako, with a white-over-red plume above a black cockade with a small gilt button in the centre. On the front, a large brass plate, which incorporated the royal cypher and the usual motto and trophies of arms. The details of the scarlet jacket have been taken from the actual garment. The dark blue collar has double gold lace loops on each side with a fine line of blue within each loop. The pattern of lace is shown here. The dark blue shoulder straps had white worsted tufts. On the front of the double-breasted jacket are two rows of eight gilt buttons grouped in pairs; all the buttons are hollowbacked and bear the engraved letters T.C.D. surmounted by a crown. Dark blue lapels were folded across the chest to show the facing colour. Each dark blue cuff had four buttons set in pairs. The white turnbacks have a dark blue heart-shaped device stitched to the base of each, and the tails have pockets concealed in horizontal slits in the lining. On the junction of the centre of the back are two buttons; directly below, on each side, is a double pair within the fold and, directly below that, a single button at the base. There are (continued on page 62)

---

1 Robert Gibbs was principally a landscape and portrait painter. He studied in Trinity College, Dublin and on leaving, went to live in Cork where he practised as a presbyterian minister. He eventually emigrated to Australia where he died in 1837.
2 Often carried on the arm and known as a Chapeau Bras.
3 A rather amusing incident in the history of the corps is recorded concerning a review in

Phoenix Park, in which they took part. An order to fire a salute was given but, for some reason, the order to withdraw the ramrods had been overlooked. As a result, the spectators were somewhat alarmed to witness a shower of ramrods descending upon them. The corps was disbanded shortly afterwards. Dublin Civic Museum has six of the muskets used on that occasion. Needless to say, the ramrods are missing.

PLATE 24

UNIFORMS OF 1803

beltplate,
Bank Infantry

lace pattern, College Infantry

reverse, College Infantry jacket

rear cuff detail

captain, Bank Infantry

Dublin parish constable

private, College Infantry

FGT

One of the larger Yeomanry corps was the 1st Regiment Royal Dublin Volunteers, associated on 26 October 1796 and formed from the St Stephen's Green division of infantry. This division consisted of ten companies.

Fortunately the dress regulations of this corps from 1803 have survived, and it is from this valuable source that the figures in this plate are reconstructed.[1]

Private The black leather 1800-pattern shako had a white feather plume with a black cockade below and a small brass button on the centre. The scarlet[2] jacket had blue facings. There was gold lace edging on the shoulder straps and wings. On the front of the jacket were two rows of brass buttons set in pairs and each button had a crowned Maid of Erin harp on the centre with '1st' and 'Regt.' and the title 'Royal Dublin Volunteers' around the edge. There were two small buttons on the collar and four large buttons on the cuffs set in pairs. The turnbacks were white. Holding the white cross belts in place was an oval brass beltplate from the collection of the National Museum of Ireland, which had a crowned Maid of Erin harp on the centre, with '1st' and 'Regt.', and on scrolls the title 'Royal Dublin' and 'Volunteers' respectively. Below the harp the date 1796 was engraved. The belts held a black leather pouch and a bayonet scabbard. The breeches were blue with black gaiters and shoes. The Brown Bess musket had a white sling.

In the museum of the Grand Lodge of Freemasons of Ireland are the colours and drums of the regiment. The regimental colour is dark blue with the new 1801 Union flag in canton, the saltire of St Patrick's Cross now included. On the centre of the blue field is a light buff panel and, within the panel, a white representation of a Maid of Erin harp and the three castles, the arms of the city of Dublin. '1st' and 'Reg.' appear at the sides. Surrounding the panel are branches entwined and green foliate, and above on a small oval panel similarly decorated is the date 1796 in black. Below, on a buff scroll, is the title 'Royal Dublin Volunteers' set above a small wreath of roses and green leaves.

The **King's colour** shows the new Union flag to better effect. On the centre is a buff oval crest with the title 'Royal Dublin Volunteers' and within a Maid of Erin harp. A gold crown with white pearls surmounts the crest. At the base of the crest a small tablet bears the inscription '1 Reg.'. A wreath of roses and thistles surrounds the crest. Suspended from the base of the brass finial are gold and crimson cords and tassels.

The **regimental side-drum** is blue with red hoops and white tension ropes. Painted in gold is a circular disc surmounted by a crown with white pearls and a red cap. In the centre of the disc is a Maid of Erin harp with what appears to be the Prince of Wales white feather plumes. At each side are '1st' and 'Regt.' respectively and on the belt the title 'Royal Dublin Volunteers'. The sides of the disc has a trophy of arms comprising a pre-1801 Union flag,[3] two red colours, and a green gold-edged guidon, together with cannons, a drum and a trumpet.

The black felt cocked hat of an **officer** had a white feather plume held at the base by a black cockade and a gold lace loop and button. The scarlet coatee had blue facings with two rows of gilt buttons grouped in pairs; the cuffs were done in the same manner. On the right shoulder was a gold-fringed epaulette and a small button. The white shoulder belt had a gilt beltplate. The turnbacks of the coatee were white and were longer than those on the men's jackets. Around the waist was a crimson sash knotted on the left side and terminated in long tassels. Black Hessian boots were worn with blue breeches and the 1796-pattern sword had a gilt guard, a gold-lace knot and a black leather scabbard with gilt mountings.

1 This information is included in the Joly papers in the National Library. It is interesting to record that Jean Jasper, the first of the Joly family to settle in Ireland, provided a valuable link with the Volunteers of 1778 and the Yeomanry (Volunteers) of 1796. Jean Jaspar Joly was a native of Charneux in Flanders and a lineal descendant of George Joly, Baron de Blaisy of Dijon. When William Robert Fitzgerald, Marquess of Kildare, was on the grand tour he met Jean Jaspar Joly and brought him back to Ireland and employed him as his secretary in Carton. Joly subsequently joined the 1st Regiment Royal Dublin Volunteers with the rank of captain, commanded by his friend who had since become the Duke of Leinster. Two medals in the collection of the National Museum awarded to this corps give the prefix 'Royal' and are dated 1779 and 1793 respectively. Francis Wheatley's famous painting entitled 'The Dublin Volunteers in College Green, 4th November 1779' (in the National Gallery) depicts Jean Jasper, now known as John, standing behind the Duke of Leinster at the base of the statue of

William III. These Volunteers of Grattan's Parliament were abolished in 1793. When the majority of Yeomanry corps were raised in 1796, John Jasper Joly joined the new 1st Regiment Royal Dublin Volunteers and was commissioned 3rd Lieutenant on 13 September 1798; his captain's rank in the former movement carried no weight. He was friendly with Lord Edward Fitzgerald and his successors distinguished themselves in Irish life over the years. He died on 13 December 1825 and is buried in Old St Kevin's Church, Camden Row, Dublin. His most recent successor, the late Jaspar Joly, who died in 1988, supplied the writer with invaluable information.

2 It was quite common for the other ranks of Yeomanry corps to wear scarlet instead of red as the vast majority would have had private means.

3 There is also a base drum in the same collection. The Union flag in this case is the post-1801 version, and the hoops are red and blue.

PLATE 25
YEOMANRY INFANTRY, 1803: 1ST REGIMENT, ROYAL DUBLIN VOLUNTEERS

private

officer

regimental colour

King's colour

side-drum

beltplate

button

In 1794, two Fencible cavalry regiments were raised in Ireland – the 1st Fencible Dragoons and the 2nd Fencible Dragoons.[1] They were both light dragoon corps by virtue of the uniforms they wore. Of particular interest is the first-named regiment, also known as the Irish Foxhunters, which was raised by the Earl of Roden on 21 July 1794 and disbanded on 7 October 1800. Fortunately the two standards of this corps have survived, and it is thanks to the present Earl of Roden that illustrations of these could be made.

The field of the standard shown top left is light buff with a gold crowned Maid of Erin harp[2] set on a red background as a centrepiece. The crown has a red cap within and the harp is surrounded by a wreath of roses, thistles and green foliate; at the base is a small white bow. In each corner is an oval red panel bordered by an ornamental white design. The top left and bottom right panels contain floral designs incorporating a thistle and a rose and green leaves. The top right and bottom left panels contain the white horse of Hanover.

In the standard shown bottom left the field is the same colour as previously described. The centrepiece contains a thistle and rose with respective leaves,

surmounted by a gold crown. Below, set on a red scroll and embroidered in gold is the royal motto DIEU ET MON[3] DROIT. The scroll is edged white. The four oval panels are the same dimensions as on the other standard; top right and bottom left bear the white horse of Hanover. The top left and bottom right bear the gold embroidered inscriptions '1st Fens L.D.' (1st Fencibles Light Dragoons), which leaves one in no doubt as to the nature of the regiment.

Charles Hamilton Smith's[4] sketchbooks contain drawings of the uniforms of both these regiments. The 1st Fencibles have dark blue jackets, with white facings, lace and breeches. The helmets are fur-crested with a white turban and a red and white feather plume.

In Monaghan County Museum is a regimental colour of a Yeomanry infantry corps, titled 'Farney Yeomen'.[5]

The colour shown on the right is a pinkish red with the pre-1801 Union flag in canton. The green central panel is edged gold with a crowned Maid of Erin harp, the letters G.R., and the title 'Farney Yeomen', all worked in gold.

---

1 The 2nd Fencible Dragoons were raised by Lord Glentworth, later Earl of Limerick on 4 August 1794 and were disbanded on 15 September 1800. According to Hamilton Smith's sketch books, their uniform was the same as the 1st Regiment, except that their facings and turbans were yellow.

2 It is worth noting that the harp is placed in the opposite direction with the female figure facing to the right, instead of to the more usual left.

3 Note the position of the letter N.

4 The works of Lt-Col. Charles Hamilton Smith (1776-1859), now in the Victoria and Albert Museum, include many illustrations on military and civilian costume of this period.

5 Farney is a barony in South County Monaghan, with Carrickmacross as the chief town. In 1803, the Farney Infantry had two companies. The name of H. Evatt appears as the captain of both companies; the combined strength was 219 all ranks.

PLATE 26
LOYALIST FLAGS

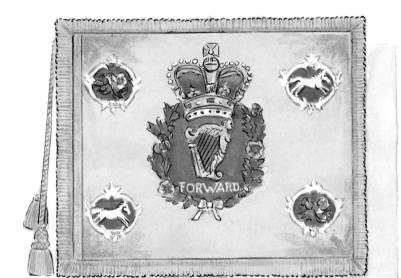

1st Fencible Dragoons
second standard (obverse)

Another 1st Fencible
Dragoons
first standard (reverse)

Farney Yeomen Infantry regimental colour, 1796-1801

From page 24

A sergeant of the 17th or Royal Meath Regiment had a uniform which was basically the same as in Plate 7, with the following exceptions. The facings were blue on account of the regiment's royal prefix; on the right shoulder, a silver-lace epaulette and fringes, and around the waist a crimson sash knotted at the left side with a central blue stripe to match the facings on the coat. A white shoulder belt with a brass beltplate held the sword. In 1792 sergeants were issued with pikes in place of the previous halberds. The pike was nine feet in length, with a steel crossbar below the blade and a steel tip at the base of the wooden shaft.

From page 42

rosettes placed around the top edge. Their long coats were light-blue and decorated with white lace, the colours of Dublin City. This blue was relieved by a dark-red collar and hose. On the breast and the back below a lace design, a divided shield was worn, containing a harp on one side and the three castles or watchtowers on the other side. Below the belt on the skirts the letters C.D. (Corporation or City of Dublin) were placed. The shoes were black. The small sword had a black grip and a brass guard, a blade two feet six inches in length, and a brown scabbard with a brass tip. The partizan, no doubt referred to as an axe, had a long green-and-white tassel at the base of the steel blade. The shaft was dark oak with a steel tip. Examples of both these weapons are in the collection of the Dublin Civic Museum. It would appear that the officer commanding this Guard wore a conventional eighteenth-century-style blue coat with waistcoat and breeches of the same colour, all laced with silver, together with a black cocked hat and red hose. It is not known when this Guard was discontinued, but it was much in evidence, along with the Battle Axe Guards, during the visit of George IV in 1821.

From page 48

of the Most Noble Order of the Garter; this was worn under the coat). Finally a wooden rod with a cord and tassel and a steel tip.

Officer of the 6th Foot (centre company) The 6th (1st Warwickshire) Regiment of Foot was one of the few regular infantry regiments actively employed in Ireland. Its origins was one of the 'Holland Regiments' which returned with William of Orange to England in 1688, having been in Dutch service for fifteen years prior to that date.

The black cocked hat was edged with silver lace and had a loop and a small button on a black cockade. The scarlet coat had deep yellow facings and silver buttons grouped in pairs. On each button the numeral 6 appears on the centre with an attractive design around the edge. The shoulder belt plate was silver and the gorget gilt since 1796, in place of the previous silver. A silver-laced fringed epaulette was worn on the right shoulder and, around the waist, a crimson sash knotted on the left side.

From page 50

The leopardskin shabraque had a wide band of gold lace and buff scalloped edges. The bridle was of the Hungarian pattern. All the straps were black leather and all buckles, studs, stirrups and metal ornamentation were gilt.

Theobald Wolfe Tone was appointed adjutant-general to the Army of Sambre et Meuse, under the command of General Hoche, in February 1797. He is depicted wearing undress uniform, or 'petit uniforme'.

The blue coatee was relieved by a high red collar with a row of gold oak leaf embroidery around the top and front edges; this was the rank insignia for brigadier-generals as adjutant-general was an appointment. Below the black stock, a white frill was visible. On the front of the coatee was a double row of gilt buttons and a pair of gold lace fringed epaulettes, devoid of rank markings[3] and each held in place by a small gilt button. The wide sash knotted at the left side was a brigadier-general's distinction. This was medium blue with interwoven gold thread terminating in two large gold tassels. Light leather gauntlets, popular with citizen generals, obscured the cuffs which were decorated with a single row of gold oak leaves as on the collar. Swords of the Mameluke pattern for generals had not been officially approved until 1799, so a rather classical pattern was carried. Its black grip had a gilt guard and pommel and a gold lace knot; the black scabbard had gilt mountings and rings richly ornamented with classical designs. The slings were gold lace. The breeches were white with an option for blue on other occasions. Boots were black with brown tops and gilt spurs. The black felt bicorn hat had gold lace edging, loop and gilt button which held the tricolour cockade in place.

From page 56

two three-pointed slashes, each with four buttons set in pairs. The white cross-belts held the usual black leather pouch and bayonet. The breeches were white with black gaiters worn over black shoes. The Brown Bess musket was the principal weapon carried. Officers of the College Infantry would have worn the cocked hat with a more ornate jacket.

---

3 Rank insignia consisting of two stars for brigadier-generals was introduced *c*.1802.

SOURCES

Barthorp, Michael, *British Cavalry Uniforms since 1660* (Poole, 1984).

Brunskill, H.O., *A Short History of the Irish Parliament House, now the Bank of Ireland* (Dublin, 1934).

Burton, Rev. Nathanael, *History of the Royal Hospital, Kilmainham, near Dublin, from the Original Foundation to the Present Time* (Dublin, 1843).

Carman, W.Y., *Richard Simkin's Uniforms of the British Army, the Cavalry Regiments* (Exeter, 1982).

Chichester, Henry Manners and Burges-Short, George, *Records and Badges of Every Regiment and Corps in the British Army* (London, 1900).

Correspondence of the author with Colonel Paul Willing, formerly of Hotel National des Invalides, Musée de l'Armée, Paris; Monsieur Jean Pré, Meudon, France; and Marcel Roubíček of Prague.

Crooks, Major J.J., *History of the Royal Irish Regiment of Artillery* (Dublin, 1914).

Dawnay, Major N.P., *The Distinction of Rank of Regimental Officers, 1684 to 1855*, Society for Army Historical Research, Special Publication No. 7 (Army Museums Ogilby Trust, Aldershot, 1960).

De Marbot and Dunoyer de Noirmont, *Costumes Militaires Françaises* (Paris c.1869), iii, Plate No. 52, and text.

Forde, Frank, 'The Royal Irish Artillery, 1755-1801', *Irish Sword*, XI, Summer 1973.

Fosten, Bryan, 'The Regiments Von Hompesch' *Airfix Magazine* (Cambridge, c.1976) plate 17.

—, *Wellington's Infantry* (2) (London, 1982).

—, *Wellington's Light Cavalry* (London, 1982).

Hayes-McCoy, G.A., 'The Irish Pike', *Journal of the Galway Archaeological & Historical Society*, XX, nos. iii & iv, 1943.

—, *Irish Battles. A Military History of Ireland* (Belfast, 1990).

—, 'The Red Coat and the Green' Studies, XXXVII, no. 148, December, 1948.

—, *A History of Irish Flags from Earliest Times* (Dublin, 1979).

Funcken, Liliane et Fred, *L'Uniforme et les Armes des Soldats du Premier Empire* (Tournai, 1968).

Haythornthwaite, Philip, *Weapons & Equipment of the Napoleonic Wars* (Poole, Dorset, 1979).

—, *Uniforms of the French Revolutionary Wars 1789-1802* (Poole, Dorset, 1989).

Kenny, Michael, *The 1798 Rebellion. Photographs and Memorabilia from the National Museum of Ireland* (Town House and Country House, Dublin 1996).

Lawson, Cecil C.P., *A History of the Uniforms of the British Army*, iii (London, 1961), iv (London, 1970) and v (London, 1967).

MacDonald, Captain R.J., *The History of the Dress of the Royal Regiment of Artillery, 1625-1897* (London, 1899; reprinted by Crecy Books, Bristol, 1985).

McAnally, Sir Henry, *The Irish Militia, 1793-1816* (Dublin and London, 1949).

McDonnell, J., *Buttons of the Irish Militia 1793-1881* (Dublin, 1991).

Parkyn, Major H.G., *Shoulder-Belt Plates and Buttons* (Aldershot, 1956).

Scobie, Captain I.H. MacKay, *An Old Highland Fencible Corps. The History of the Reay Fencible Highland Regiment of Foot, or MacKay's Highlanders, 1794-1802, with an account of its services in Ireland during the Rebellion of 1798* (Edinburgh and London, 1914).

The Scottish Clans and their Tartans, Thirty-sixth edition (Edinburgh and London).

Thorburn, W.A., *French Army Regiments & Uniforms from the Revolution to 1870* (London, 1969).

Thompson, F. Glenn, 'Theobald Wolfe Tone – Adjutant General', *An Cosantóir*, July 1989.

—, 'The Bank of Ireland Yeomanry', *Irish Sword*, XIV, no. 57, 1981.

—, 'A Coatee of the Trinity College Yeomanry', *Irish Sword*, XVII, no. 66, 1987.

Wheeler, H.F.B. and Broadley, A.M., *The War in Wexford. An account of the Rebellion in the south of Ireland in 1798* (London, 1910).

Wilkinson-Latham, Robert, *Swords in Colour* (Poole, Dorset, 1977).